The Baby-led Weaning Cookbook

13

Published in 2010 by Vermilion, an imprint of
Ebury Publishing

Ebury Publishing is a Random House Group
company

The Random House Group Limited Reg. No. 954009

Addresses for companies within the Random House
Group can be found at www.randomhouse.co.uk

A CIP catalogue record for this book is available
from the British Library

Penguin Random House is committed to a
sustainable future for our business, our readers
and our planet. This book is made from Forest
Stewardship Council® certified paper.

MIX
Paper from
responsible sources
FSC® C018179
www.fsc.org

Printed and bound in Italy by Printer Trento S.r.l.
ISBN 9780091935283

Copies are available at special rates for bulk orders.
Contact the sales development team on 020 7840
8487 for more information.

To buy books by your favourite authors and register
for offers, visit www.randomhouse.co.uk

The information in this book has been compiled by
way of general guidance in relation to the specific
subjects addressed, but is not a substitute and not to
be relied on for medical, healthcare, pharmaceutical
or other professional advice on specific circumstances
and in specific locations. Parents are advised to
consult their health visitor, GP or other relevant
healthcare practitioner if they are concerned about
their baby's health or development and before
changing, stopping or starting any medical treatment.
So far as the authors are aware the information given
is correct and up to date as at May 2010. Practice,
laws, regulations and recommendations all change,
and the reader should obtain up-to-date professional
advice on any such issues. The authors and
publishers disclaim, as far as the law allows, any
liability arising directly or indirectly from the use,
or misuse, of the information contained in this book.

Photo credits
Pages 9, 11, 14, 31, 32, back cover far left and
back cover centre right © Caroline Gue (of CP
Photography); pages 23, 24 and 27 © Shaun Murkett;
page 10 © David Payne; front cover © Janice
Milnerwood; back cover centre left and back cover
centre right © Shutterstock

Thank you to the parents of these babies, for
permission to use their photographs: Chloe Stanwick,
7 months (pages 4 and 38); Arthur Gue, 6, 9 and
12 months (pages 9, 11, 14, 31, 32, back cover far
left and back cover centre right); Isabelle Dammery,
7 months (page 10); Santiago Baldessari, 6 months
(page 15); Finn Warren, 6 months (page 21);
Sophie Livings, 10 months (pages 23 and 27);
Elsie Rweyemamu, 8½ months (page 24); Max
Kellas-Mabbott, 10 months (page 26); Amy Spencer,
6½ months (page 30)

The Baby-led Weaning Cookbook

Over 130 delicious recipes for the whole family to enjoy

GILL RAPLEY & TRACEY MURKETT

Vermilion
LONDON

Contents

Introduction

If you like the idea of introducing your baby to the pleasure of family mealtimes and sharing good, healthy food, then *The Baby-led Weaning Cookbook* is for you. It's about making simple, nutritious meals so that your baby can join you at the table and feed himself when he is ready, eating what everyone else is eating.

If you haven't yet read our first book, *Baby-led Weaning*, and baby-led weaning is new to you, the first few chapters of this book will introduce you to the basics.

Your baby's first experiences of solid food won't be puréed 'baby food', spoon-fed to him by someone else. Instead he'll pick up pieces of real food himself, feel them in his hand, sniff them, taste them and – gradually – learn to eat them.

Starting solids this way is easy, enjoyable and stress-free for the whole family. It is part of your baby's natural development, giving him the chance to learn new skills and grow in confidence. Sharing your own meals with your baby is quicker than preparing separate purées and cheaper than buying them ready-made. And it's much more fun.

This isn't a book full of 'finger foods'; all the recipes – with their rich variety of taste and textures, from Colourful Stir-fry Salad to Shepherd's Pie – can be adapted easily so that your baby will be able to join in, even when he is just getting started. Nothing has to be cut into smiley shapes to 'tempt' him, and there are no 'hidden' vegetables to trick him. It's good family food that your baby can share and everyone will enjoy.

The dishes are easy to make, tasty and nutritious, but they aren't 'ours'; they have come from other baby-led weaning parents who wanted to share ideas for food that worked well for them and their baby. They are favourite meals, tried and tested.

If you've never cooked a meal from scratch before, or if you're just not very confident in the kitchen, the recipes are easy to follow, and there are some helpful tips on basic techniques. If you're already an experienced home cook, this book will provide inspiration for great meals that will work easily with baby-led weaning.

Our aim is to give you the confidence to make a real variety of delicious meals so that you can share good, healthy food with your baby and make family mealtimes the pleasure they should be.

Note: Throughout the book we have tried to be fair to boys and girls by alternating the use of he and she in the chapters. No difference between girls and boys is implied.

Part One
Baby-led Weaning

'I love having my two children sitting next to me with us all eating the same food. I just make healthy meals and Elliot joins in – he'll have a go at anything. There's no stress and he really enjoys it.'

Rikke, mother of Elliot, 11 months, and Ruben, 2 years

Chapter One
BABY-LED WEANING BASICS

Eating with your baby – at the same time, at the same table and sharing the same food – is at the heart of baby-led weaning. There is no need for 'baby food', purées or spoon feeding. Your baby simply feeds herself, exploring and enjoying healthy family meals, from her very first taste of solid food. Baby-led weaning (BLW) makes introducing solids easier and more enjoyable for the whole family and encourages your baby to become confident and happy at mealtimes and to enjoy good, nutritious food as she grows up.

The principle of baby-led weaning is based on the way babies develop and the skills that appear naturally in their first year. If parents give their baby the opportunity to handle food at about the right time, she will instinctively start to feed herself when she is ready. For most babies, this happens at around six months old, which is the same age that the UK Departments of Health and the World Health Organization recommend that babies should start on solid foods. The baby then progresses at her own pace, cutting down her milk feeds when she is ready.

This is very different from the conventional approach, in which the parents make the decision to start their baby on solids, beginning with spoon-fed purées and steering her through set stages towards eventually joining in family meals – something that often doesn't happen until well into toddlerhood.

Of course, babies helping themselves to family food isn't new; it's what babies seem to do naturally. Many parents, especially those who have several children, have spotted their baby grabbing something from someone else's plate and happily munching away on it. They quickly realise that letting her feed herself as soon as she can makes mealtimes easier and more enjoyable for everyone. And for generations, parents have been encouraged to give their babies finger foods from six months onwards, to help them to develop chewing skills. What is changing now is the assumption that babies need to get used to purées before they can move on to finger foods. This isn't the case. Sucking puréed food from a spoon doesn't prepare babies for chewing; the best way to develop chewing skills is to practise them on food that actually needs chewing – in other words, ordinary, un-mashed food.

'We tried to start Thomas on solids by giving him mush – but he'd just clamp his mouth shut. He was so much happier when he could pick up pieces of food himself. He's always been a fiercely independent little person.'
Elizabeth, mother of Thomas, 13 months

Why Spoon Feeding is Unnecessary

Most people still take it for granted that spoon feeding is the normal way to give babies their first solid foods. But, like much of the current advice on introducing solids, spoon feeding is left over from the days when parents were advised to start solids at three or four months of age – when their babies were too young to feed themselves.

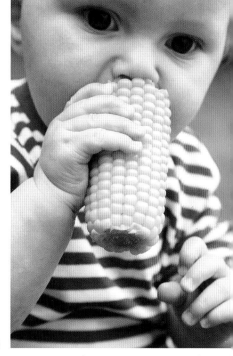

We now know that babies don't need solid foods, and their bodies aren't really ready for them, until they are around six months old. If you've waited until six months to start solids with your baby, you've skipped the spoon-feeding stage. At this age babies are quite capable of feeding themselves and they don't need to be spoon fed. In fact, many parents find their baby of six months refuses to be fed by someone else; they want to handle food themselves because their instincts drive them to find out about things by testing them out with their hands and mouths.

'I gave Will some couscous for the first time today. It was fascinating watching him work out how to get it to his mouth. He seemed to learn a completely new skill in the space of one meal!'
Karen, mother of Sam, 2 years, and Will, 8 months

What Happens with BLW

The first few months of BLW are not really about eating – they're about exploring food. Your baby will start by handling food, learning what it looks and feels like, then she'll use her mouth to discover its taste and texture. She may not actually eat any at first, but this is quite normal; her milk feeds (whether she is breast- or formula fed) are still providing almost all of her nutrition so she doesn't need anything else yet.

This is what happens typically in BLW:

- The baby is included in family mealtimes, where she watches what others are doing and is offered the chance to join in.
- Nobody 'feeds' the baby; when she is ready she starts handling food and taking it to her mouth herself (at first with her fingers, and later with cutlery).
- To start with, food is offered in pieces that are easy to pick up (babies soon learn how to handle a range of sizes, shapes and textures).
- It's up to the baby how much she eats, and how fast she eats it. It's also up to her how quickly she moves on to a wider range of foods.
- The baby continues to have milk feeds (breast milk or formula) whenever she wants them and she decides when she is ready to begin reducing them.

Key Benefits of BLW

Going *with* your baby's instinct to handle food, rather than *against* it, makes weaning easier and more fun than doing things the conventional way – but there are many other benefits to taking a baby-led approach. It's great for babies because it:

- Allows each baby to move on to solid foods at the right time and pace for her developing body, and ensures that her important milk feeds are not cut out too early
- Allows babies to explore the taste, texture, colour and smell of individual foods

- Helps to develop babies' hand-eye coordination, dexterity and chewing skills
- Allows each baby to eat as much as she needs, in her own time, so establishing good eating habits that may last a lifetime (and which may help to avoid obesity and other food-related problems)
- Makes picky eating and mealtime battles less likely (when there is no pressure on babies to eat, there is far less opportunity for meals to become a battleground)
- Encourages confidence at mealtimes and enjoyment of a wide range of foods
- Means babies can be part of family mealtimes from the beginning

Baby-led weaning is great for parents too because it means more relaxed mealtimes for the whole family. There's no pressure to get your baby to eat and no need for games or tricks to persuade her to eat healthy foods. And you don't need to make or buy purées, so eating in is cheaper and eating out is easier. Plus, of course, eating with those we love is an enormously important way of developing and cementing strong family bonds.

Is BLW Suitable for all Babies?

Some babies have medical or developmental problems that prevent them from picking up food, or from chewing it. Others, who were born prematurely, may need solid foods before they are physically able to feed themselves. If this is the case for your baby, she may need to be spoon fed, at least at first. But, as long as it's safe, it is still a good idea to encourage her to handle food, to help her to develop some of the skills that she finds difficult. If you are in any doubt about your baby's general health or development, seek advice from a doctor or dietitian before you start offering solid foods.

'We decided early on that mealtimes were going to be a social thing, not just about the food. It really took the pressure off eating, and, now he's older, Daniel joins in with our conversations and mealtimes are just great.'
Lisa, mother of Daniel, 2 years

Chapter Two
HOW BABIES LEARN TO FEED THEMSELVES

Babies learn to feed themselves with solid foods naturally, when the time is right, but it can be useful to know when your baby is likely to be ready and how his skills will develop. This chapter explains what to look for and how you can help your baby to progress at his own pace.

The Right Time for Solids

For the first six months of their lives all babies need is breast milk or infant formula, which are full of easily digested nutrients and calories. Their digestive and immune systems aren't yet ready to cope with anything else.

Milk feeds continue to provide almost all of a baby's nutrition until they are about one year old, but from around six months they start to need more nutrients than they can get from milk alone. However, the need is very small at first and grows quite slowly, so there is no reason to rush the introduction of solid foods. Most babies require only very small quantities of solid food until they are between nine months and a year old. They need time to get used to the feel and taste of food, and for their bodies to adjust naturally, before they eat more.

A baby's gradual need for more nutrients develops at the same pace as his skill at getting food to his mouth and his body's ability to cope with it. If he is allowed to feed himself from the beginning, he'll spend the first few months of family meals learning how to handle food (with his hands and his mouth), while his body gradually adapts to a mixed diet. So by the time he actually needs to eat more – between about nine months and a year – he will be able to feed himself a wide variety of foods and his eating will become more purposeful. It's only then that he'll gradually start to cut down his milk intake.

Is My Baby Ready?

The UK Departments of Health's recommended minimum age for starting solid foods is six months; a few babies may be ready a week or two earlier, and it's not unusual for some babies not to be really interested in eating until they are eight months or older. The problem for parents is that most of the signs of readiness they have traditionally been told to watch out for (such as waking at night) appear considerably earlier than six months. We now know that these are not linked to the need for extra nutrients or to the ability to digest other foods – they're just things that happen naturally. Extra hungriness isn't a sign of readiness either: if a baby needs fuel for growth, then calorie-dense breast milk (or formula) is the answer, not solid foods.

Most babies are only truly ready to start exploring solid foods when they can do all of the following:

- Sit up with little or no support
- Reach out and grab things effectively
- Take objects to their mouth quickly and accurately
- Make gnawing and chewing movements

These signs usually appear together at around six months – rarely much earlier. But the most reliable sign is when your baby grabs food from your plate and takes it to his mouth and starts to chew it.

'I was peeling an orange one day and Rae was literally trying to climb out of her highchair to grab it from me. I gave her it and she loved it.'
Lucy, mother of Natalie, 3 years, and Rae, 8 months

Moving Towards Solid Food

Just like learning to smile, crawl, walk or talk, learning to eat solid food is a natural part of any healthy baby's development. These key skills always develop in the same order, but at each baby's unique pace. So, although these abilities emerge at a slightly different time for each baby, the skills they need have all been developing gradually, from birth onwards.

A healthy, full-term baby can find his way to his mother's breast and feed as soon as he is born. The mother helps by holding her baby in a supportive position but the rest is done by the baby himself – self-feeding starts from the very beginning. This is a fundamental survival skill that all newborn babies have, even if they're not breastfed. If the baby is allowed to feed whenever he needs to, he will manage his own appetite and take exactly the amount he needs.

By around four months the baby is beginning to develop skills that will later help

him to eat solid food. He can reach out and grab hold of interesting things (his toys or someone's keys, for example) and he is starting to bring them to his mouth so that he can explore them with his lips and tongue. Babies' mouths are extremely sensitive and this is how they learn about taste, texture, shape and size.

By around six months, the baby is able to take things to his mouth more accurately. If he picks up something edible, he'll treat it just like a toy – he'll explore it with his hands (which are more coordinated now) and his mouth, but he doesn't know it's food. *He is curious, rather than hungry.* If he manages to get some into his mouth, that, for him, is an interesting bonus, but not the purpose of the exercise.

The ability to chew also begins to develop at around six months. This is an important skill because chewing food (with or without teeth) softens it and mixes it with saliva, which makes it easier and safer to swallow, and it also begins the process of digestion. Having the opportunity to practise chewing as early as possible is the best way to ensure that babies learn to do it effectively. Babies who aren't given the opportunity to chew food until they are quite a bit older than six months (10 months or more) are often fussy eaters later on.

Because eating skills develop in a pre-set order, babies discover how to gum, gnaw, bite and chew food before they learn to move anything to the back of their throat for swallowing. This means that they rarely try to swallow anything that they haven't chewed. So don't be surprised if, for the first week or two of solid foods, much of what your baby appears to be eating doesn't actually get swallowed but instead falls back out of his mouth.

'We offered Dylan some apple and pear for his first solids. We were so impressed with how accurately he managed to coordinate his hands to get the fruit into his mouth – he definitely wouldn't have been able to do that even a few weeks ago. He seemed to really enjoy trying both. Not sure much was actually eaten though!'
Louise, mother of Dylan, 6 months

The gag reflex

Many babies gag when they are learning to manage solid food in their mouths. It may be that this is a way of helping them to learn to eat safely, by teaching them not to overfill their mouths or to push food too far back before they've chewed it. Some babies gag only once or twice, while others continue to do it on and off for several weeks.

When a baby gags, food that isn't ready to be swallowed is pushed forward in a retching movement to prevent it getting to the back of the throat. In a baby, the gag reflex is very sensitive, so it is activated more easily than in an adult, with the 'trigger point' much farther forward in the mouth.

Although gagging can be unsettling to watch, most babies don't seem to be bothered by it; they usually bring the offending piece of food forward fairly quickly, then either spit it out or chew it – and carry on eating quite happily.

To help the gag reflex to work for your baby, make sure that he is sitting upright while he is eating (supported if necessary), so that any food that isn't ready for swallowing falls forward – out of his mouth – rather than sliding backwards towards his throat. It's also important that no-one but your baby puts food into his mouth, so that he can take the time he needs to control each mouthful effectively.

Although they are sometimes confused, choking is not the same as gagging; choking happens when something completely or partially blocks the airway (way past where the gag reflex is triggered). A total blockage is very rare (and requires standard first-aid measures) but babies can usually cough up something that is partially blocking their airway very well by themselves, provided they are sitting upright or leaning forward. Choking is no more likely with baby-led weaning than with spoon feeding, provided simple, basic safety rules are followed, See page 33 for more information on safety.

Helping Your Baby to Learn

Babies need lots of opportunities to practise their eating skills and a range of foods to learn on. That way they can work out how to manage different textures and gradually increase the amount they eat by themselves. There is no need for the traditional 'stages', where you start with a few teaspoons of smooth purée and progress, eventually, to lumpy foods three times a day.

However, it is possible to pinpoint a few key eating skills that appear as your baby progresses and this can be a useful way to make sure you are giving him all the opportunities he needs to learn and to widen his diet. The grid opposite and overleaf identifies what to look for and roughly how old your baby will be when these skills start to appear.

It's a good idea to prepare your meals so that they include textures and shapes that your baby hasn't quite mastered yet, alongside food he can manage fairly easily. Since most meals have a variety of shapes and textures, the easiest way to do this is simply to share all the different elements of your meal with your baby. As long as you include food he *can* manage, he will be able to try out the rest without getting frustrated. In fact, he will probably surprise you with what he can do, if you give him the opportunity.

Each skill will appear at the time that is right for your baby, so any attempt to teach him or push him is likely to be frustrating for both of you. He will learn to eat with a fork or a spoon eventually, but most babies find that fingers are the most efficient method for quite a while. If you concentrate on giving your baby the opportunity to try out different skills, he'll enjoy developing them in his own time.

'Eddie now wants to put a spoon in the bowl and get the food himself. He's always been pretty good at aiming with a spoon, but hasn't quite got the coordination to get it from the bowl yet – but he's on his way.'

Rachel, mother of Robin, 2½ years, and Eddie, 11 months

Developing Skills

Ready to start: From around 6 months

What you'll see

He can take toys to his mouth accurately and quickly. He gnaws on them and makes chewing movements. He is able to sit up straight with little support and will probably want to join you at the table. He may grab a large piece of food from your plate and take it to his mouth.

Easy to manage foods

Large stick-shaped pieces of food, including fruit and vegetables (see page 25), crusts, toast, large pasta shapes and soft patties or rissoles shaped or cut into 'fingers'. Long strips of meat.

Foods for him to try

See left.

Reach and grasp, with palmar grip: From around 6–8 months

What you'll see

He can reach out for large pieces of food and grasp them, using his whole hand. But he can't get at the food once it's inside his fist, so he needs it to be long enough to poke out of the top, so he can gum or gnaw it. He may hold the food in one hand and use the other hand to guide it to his mouth. He doesn't yet know his own strength, so he tends to crush soft foods in his hands. In the early weeks most food falls out of his mouth because he hasn't yet learnt to chew and swallow. He drops the food he's holding when he wants to pick up another piece because he can't yet release the food on purpose.

He spends time examining food, passing it from hand to hand and playing with it.

Easy to manage foods

Large stick-shaped pieces of food, including fruit and vegetables (see page 25), crusts, toast, large pasta shapes and soft patties or rissoles shaped or cut into 'fingers'. Long strips of meat.

Foods for him to try

Foods for picking up in clumps, such as sticky rice, thick porridge, mashed potatoes, minced meat, grated cheese. Slippery foods, such as pasta shapes with sauce.

Fist opening and closing: From around 7–9 months

What you'll see

He may be able to grab a fistful of food without too much squishing. Then, when he gets the food to his mouth, he can open his hand and push most of it in. He may also squeeze food into his mouth from his fist.

He will probably be getting better at biting and chewing. He may be happy to try a spoon or stick of food as a 'dipper' for dipping into soft or runny food, or able to manage a spoon that has been pre-loaded with food by you. He continues to examine food closely and experiment with it.

Easy to manage foods

Stick shapes and clumpy foods, as on page 17. Smaller, soft foods, such as strawberries and chunks of cooked vegetables. Slightly crunchier fruits and vegetables (depending on teeth).

Foods for him to try

Runny foods to 'dip' into, such as hummus, yoghurt, thick soups. Sticks of raw vegetables for dipping. Different shapes of pasta, such as spaghetti or tagliatelle.

Using fingers: From around 8–10 months

What you'll see

He may be able to use a 'dipper' and pick up and hold pieces of food with his fingers, without having to use his palm. He makes careful selections of what to eat, and in what order. He may want to have a go with cutlery, maybe even scooping food with a spoon or using a fork to try to stab whole pieces.

Easy to manage foods

Most stick shapes, clumpy foods and soft foods. Crunchier foods (depending on teeth). Runny foods, with a dipper.

Foods for him to try

Loose foods and small pieces, such as rice, peas, raisins and crumbly breads. Smaller chunks of food for stabbing with a fork, and soft foods to try scooping with a spoon.

Refined pincer grip: From around 9–12 months

What you'll see	*Easy to manage foods*	*Foods for him to try*
He can pick up very small pieces of food with the tip of his thumb and forefinger. He manages single grains of rice and finds the smallest crumbs! He may be starting to stab accurately with a fork and to scoop with a spoon. He may be beginning to play with food less and to eat larger amounts more purposefully.	Pretty much everything!	A full variety of textures and shapes, so that he can work out how to manage them with cutlery.

Using cutlery: From around 11–14 months

What you'll see	*Easy to manage foods*	*Foods for him to try*
He may want to use cutlery most of the time, making mealtimes very slow. He probably finds a fork easier than a spoon for getting hold of pieces of food, but he may also prefer to go back to using his fingers every now and then.	Everything.	A full variety of textures and shapes.

Chapter Three
HOW TO DO BABY-LED WEANING

Baby-led weaning may be instinctive for your baby but it is a different way of doing things for many parents. This chapter offers some ideas to help you get started and explains what to expect.

Eating Together

Babies of around five or six months are naturally curious and love to be included in any activity. So your baby is probably already letting you know that she wants to join in with mealtimes. She may not be ready for food quite yet but she wants to know what the colours, noises, smells and movements are all about.

At first, your baby may be happy to sit near you or on your knee and play with a spoon or a cup while you eat, but once she starts handling food it's important to make sure she's as upright as possible. In practice, this means sitting her either on your lap facing the table, or securely in a highchair – adjusting the straps and, if necessary, using rolled-up towels or small cushions to support her – so that she can move her arms and hands freely. And don't forget to wash her hands before she touches any food!

'It started off as a distraction technique really – I was trying to eat my dinner and Morag wasn't happy playing with spoons – she kept trying to grab stuff from my plate. So I gave her some cucumber, just so I could carry on eating, but I didn't think she'd eat any. It was a week before she was six months. But she managed to get some to her mouth and she seemed really happy.'
Lydia, mother of Caitlin, 3 years, and Morag, 12 months

Mealtimes as playtimes

For the first few months of BLW, mealtimes are like playtimes for babies. This means they should be fun, of course, but also that, from your baby's point of view, they are a serious business – because it's through playing that she learns, develops new skills and fine-tunes her coordination.

It doesn't matter if your baby eats very little in the beginning, or if she misses a meal occasionally – this is normal. Both her nourishment and her hunger are still being satisfied almost entirely by her milk feeds (see page 22). The food you give her to play with should be nutritious, because she is learning about tastes and what to expect, but mealtimes aren't really about eating at this stage.

Sharing mealtimes

With BLW there are no schedules to follow – you simply include your baby as often as possible whenever you have a meal so that she has plenty of opportunity to explore food, and to eat when she is ready.

In the early months mealtimes don't need to coincide with your baby's hunger because she isn't relying on solid food for her nourishment; it's curiosity that makes her want to join in – she won't make the link between solid foods and a full tummy for a few months yet. In fact, as with any playtime, it's best to choose a time when she *isn't* hungry. It's also best to choose a time when she isn't tired; that way she'll be able to concentrate on taking in all the new sensations and practising new skills. If she *is* hungry or tired she's likely to get frustrated and upset so, if she seems to need it, offer her a milk feed (breast or formula) or let her have a nap before sitting her up at the table with you.

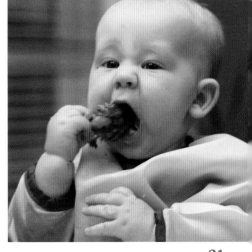

Some babies have very set routines and may be fast asleep at family mealtimes; others may still be having so many naps a day it's hard to see where any meals will fit in. If your baby is too sleepy to bother with food when you are ready to eat, it may be worth saving some of your meal and sharing it with her when she is more alert, then gradually changing either her nap times or your mealtimes.

When it isn't possible for your baby to share a mealtime with the family, make sure that someone is able to sit down to eat with her, so that she isn't eating alone.

'Family mealtimes are great. We changed our routines so we could all eat together – we eat much earlier now. And there's absolutely no focus on how much Mason is eating – he's just one of us.'

Vicky, mother of Alex, 3 years, and Mason, 11 months

What Happens with Milk Feeds?

Milk feeds (breast or formula) will continue to be the most important part of your baby's diet until she is at least one year old. Solid foods simply can't provide all the nutrients and calories babies need in their first year. So it's important not to try to *replace* milk feeds yet, but to allow your baby to *add* to them with solid foods, at her own pace, so that her diet becomes gradually more varied.

All you need to do is to carry on offering the breast or bottle whenever your baby wants a feed, so she can decide when she's ready to start taking less milk. This probably won't happen until she is at least nine months old; then, as she begins to eat more at mealtimes, you'll notice that she is beginning to reduce her milk feeds herself. Some babies don't cut down noticeably until they are well past their first birthday and many babies want more milk (and fewer solids) on some days than others; there's no rush – your baby knows what she needs.

By the time your baby is about 18 months old she will be less reliant on milk feeds, although if she's breastfed she may want to continue for another year or more.

Offering Food

When you offer your baby food, it's best to put a few pieces in front of her, rather than putting it into her hand for her. This way she can choose which piece to take first and what to do with it – or, of course, whether to pick any up at all. If possible, offer foods that the rest of the family is eating (as long as they are suitable – see Chapter Four), so that your baby feels included and can copy you. She may 'play' with the food by smearing, squeezing or dropping it; she may sniff it or take it to her mouth and lick it, but she should decide whether she wants to actually eat any or not.

Most babies find plates and bowls just as interesting as food in the early days, and will experiment with them to see what they can do. Although this is interesting for your baby, it will distract her from exploring the food itself, so it may be better to offer pieces of food on a clean highchair tray or table top, rather than a plate. (Or you can buy a special placemat, with a large pocket for catching dropped food.)

Offer just one or two pieces of a few different foods to start with, to prevent your baby from being overwhelmed. Keep some in reserve, so you can offer it later if she wants more. Remember to check the food isn't too hot before offering it – tasting it is usually the most reliable way, especially if food has been microwaved, as this can produce uneven hotspots. Putting your baby's portion on a plate that has been in the freezer for a few minutes can be a good way to cool it quickly before serving.

Tastes

It's important to offer your baby a variety of tastes. Many commercial baby foods are bland or sweet but babies often like surprisingly strong-tasting or spicy food so, provided you avoid adding salt (see pages 38–40), you can offer your baby plenty of different flavours (although you may want to go easy on the chilli until you know how hot she likes her food!). That way you will be more likely to provide her with a wide range of nutrients and to encourage her to try new foods as she grows older.

'Fay loves food with plenty of taste rather than plain or bland food. She loves anything with lots of garlic or cumin especially.'

Lucy, mother of Fay, 14 months

Moving on to cutlery

Your baby will let you know when she is ready to have a go with cutlery. She may be able to dip with a spoon fairly early, but to pick food up she'll probably prefer a fork at first (provided it's not too blunt), because stabbing is a less complicated skill than scooping. Using a small, straight-sided bowl, rather than a rounded bowl, may make it easier for her to get something on to her fork (because the food won't be able to escape as easily).

For runny foods, a small pot that your baby can hold in one hand (with a spoon in the other) will mean she can use both hands together. You may prefer to offer her a pre-loaded spoon to start with, so she can practise getting it into her mouth with some food still on it! (See page 28 for more information on runny food.)

23

Preparing Food for Your Baby

In the early weeks of baby-led weaning, the pieces of food offered to your baby should be a shape, size and texture that she will be able to pick up easily. If you watch her you will get to know what she can manage and you'll be able to adapt food quickly and easily as her skills progress.

To start with, your baby will only be able to grasp things with her whole hand, using her palm rather than just her fingers. She won't be able to open her hand on purpose to get at food inside her fist so pieces of food need to be long enough for a bit to poke out and wide enough for her to grab and close her fingers around. Thick sticks and strips are ideal. She won't be able to get hold of anything small, so think big.

Once she's got going with BLW, your baby will enjoy learning how to handle other shapes and textures. Offering foods such as rice, pasta and minced meat (and even soup), alongside pieces of food she can pick up easily, will allow her to experiment and explore without getting too frustrated. Most babies are very inventive, and the more experience your baby has with foods that need different kinds of handling and chewing, the more quickly she'll learn to deal with them.

Vegetables

Vegetables such as green beans, asparagus and okra just need to be trimmed, while broccoli and cauliflower work well as florets – with a bit of stalk to provide a 'handle'. Potatoes, sweet potatoes and squashes are best cut into sticks or wedges, with some skin left on. Other large vegetables should be cut into thick stick shapes – roughly 5cm (2in) long and 1–2cm (½–¾in) wide.

Vegetables can be steamed, boiled, grilled, roasted, stir-fried or baked. They should be firm enough for your baby to hold but soft enough for her to munch, so if you usually like your vegetables with a bit of 'bite' (al dente), you may find that you need to cook them a little longer, especially if she hasn't got any teeth yet. If you cook small vegetables (such as peas) until they're soft, your baby may be able to squash together a fistful even though she can't yet pick them up on their own.

'If we have a stir-fry I'll make sure there are some big bits and just put some of them on Luke's tray. He especially enjoys whole baby sweetcorn and mangetout.'
Sharon, mother of Luke, 10 months

Salad vegetables

Cucumber can be cut into sticks and raw peppers into thick strips; celery should have the coarse strings removed. Lettuce can be offered in strips or as rolled-up leaves (although your baby is unlikely to be able to chew it effectively, she'll probably have a go). Tomatoes are usually easier for babies to deal with if halved or quartered (depending on their size); cherry tomatoes should be cut in half.

Fruit

Fruit is easier to hold when it's left unpeeled because it is less slippery. Later, when they can bite chunks off, some babies find the peel of fruits such as apples difficult to chew. Watch your baby to judge what's best. And don't worry about skin which isn't meant to be eaten (such as pineapple) – she'll soon work out which bits are edible. All fruit should be washed and any stones removed.

You can offer your baby apples and pears in halves or quarters (not in small pieces), or you can leave the fruit whole. If you leave it whole, you may want to remove the core, so that your baby can put her thumb inside to help her hold it. Choose softer varieties, which are less likely to break off in hard chunks (microwaving hard apples for a few seconds softens them). Taking a bite out of the fruit yourself first will help your baby to get started.

Fruits such as avocado, pineapple and melon are best cut into wedges; nectarines and apricots can be offered in halves or quarters. Blueberries should be crushed slightly and grapes should be cut in half. Soft berries such as strawberries and raspberries can be offered whole – your baby will enjoy learning how to hold them without crushing them.

Bananas can be offered whole but they are usually too wide for small hands to grasp easily, so it's best to cut them lengthways. If the banana is nice and ripe, try putting pressure on the top end with your finger – it should fall naturally into three long sections, which you can then cut in half. Alternatively, cut the banana in half and trim the skin back, so that the top sticks out like an ice cream from a cone.

'Ellen will chew away at an apple slice and then just spit out the skin.'
Joanne, mother of Isabella, 2 years, and Ellen, 8 months

Pasta

Forget 'baby' pasta – your baby won't be able to get hold of it yet – instead go for large pieces that she can hold with her whole hand. Twisty shapes are easier to grasp than straight shapes, and sauces stick better to them too – try conchiglioni, fusilli and rigatoni in the beginning, moving on to smaller and smoother shapes as your baby's skills develop. Spaghetti is great fun, but you may want to save it for when you have plenty of time for the cleaning up! It's best not to add oil to your pasta when cooking it because it makes it slippery. At first your baby may prefer pasta served plain, with a little sauce on the side to play with or to lick off her fingers. Once she is more experienced with food, she will be able to manage pasta and sauce together.

Rice

Ordinary long grain rice may be tricky for your baby to manage in the very early days, although rice that has been slightly overcooked tends to stick together quite well. A better alternative is sticky rice or sushi rice, or you may want to start with dishes such as Risotto (see page 142), which can be picked up in soft handfuls, or Onigiri (see page 71). Later, your baby will enjoy picking up individual grains.

> 'If we have rice I'll mix it with a sauce so it's a bit stickier and put it on a spoon, and then just put the spoon in front of Micky so he can feed himself with it. It's very messy but he really likes it.'
>
> Rosy, mother of Will, 2 years, and Micky, 11 months

Meat

Babies often enjoy sucking or gnawing on meat as soon as they start solid food. It is best offered in large strips, or on the bone. Lamb, beef and pork need to be cooked so that the meat is very tender (stewing or slow cooking is good, whereas grilling can make it more chewy). Small home-made patties or burgers are easy to handle, and after the first few weeks your baby will probably be able to pick up fistfuls of minced meat, too. If you offer your baby sausages, remove the skin first.

Chicken is easy for babies to manage. Tear strips of breast meat along the grain, rather than across, so that they stay in one piece. Leg meat tends to be juicier and firmer than breast, while drumsticks are ideal for small hands. Remember to remove any thin splint bones or loose gristle first.

Bread

Most babies find bread easier to manage if it is toasted – soft white bread in particular can stick to the roof of a baby's mouth. Flat breads, such as pitta, tortilla wraps and chapattis, are also easier to manage than 'ordinary' bread. Toast and bread can be cut into finger shapes, strips or small triangles.

Other foods

Many other nutritious foods (see Chapter Four) can be adapted easily for your baby in the early weeks – offer whatever you think she can manage. Home-made fishcakes, meatballs and patties can be made in easy-to-handle shapes, and hard cheeses, such as Cheddar, can be cut into sticks. Offer your baby a variety of shapes, sizes and textures as she progresses, but don't forget to include some easy shapes with most meals while she is learning.

Runny foods

Runny foods can be adapted so that your baby can manage them. Soups and porridge are easy to make extra thick, and soups can have rice, small pieces of bread or tiny pasta shapes added to them so that your baby can scoop up handfuls. Bread or dumplings can be served with soups and stews, while cooled smooth soups (and yoghurt) can be 'drunk' from a pot or cup.

From about eight months your baby may be able to use a dipper, such as a breadstick or stick of carrot, with runny or soft foods. A piece of celery is especially good for scooping up dips. Alternatively, you could offer her a pre-loaded spoon to hold.

Drinks

Once your baby has joined you for meals, it's a good idea to offer her water in a small open cup (shot-glass size is ideal) whenever she sits down to eat. She'll probably just want to play with it at first but if she needs it, she'll let you know, and you can help her hold it steady for drinking if necessary.

Buying a highchair

The most useful highchairs are those that come right up to the table, so that your baby can feel truly included in family mealtimes. Many can be adjusted for older children and are a good long-term investment. If you opt for one with a tray, make sure it is fairly wide with adjustable tray positions so your baby can reach her food comfortably (many highchairs are toddler-sized, with a fixed tray position). An adjustable foot-rest will also make her more stable and help her to feel secure.

You'll probably want to think about how easy a highchair is to clean, too. Simple wooden or plastic highchairs are much easier to clean than those with lots of padding – and if it has a tray, make sure it's detachable so it can be washed in the sink.

Trusting Your Baby's Appetite

Babies are able to decide how much they need to eat but their appetites can vary from day to day. Some days your baby will eat a lot, while on other days she may peck at her food or not want to eat anything solid at all. This is entirely normal and, as long as she is well, you are offering a variety of healthy foods, and she is able to have as many milk feeds as she wants, she will be well nourished.

If – once she's eating purposefully – your baby refuses food, it could be because she's teething, coming down with a cold or simply feeling upset (for example, in the first few days after mum returns to work). Some babies (and children) regularly eat a lot for a few meals and then very little for the next few days – it's just their natural pattern.

It's important not to push your baby to eat more than she wants. If you were brought up to believe children should make a 'clean plate', offering her a very small portion (with more available if she wants it), may help you to resist coaxing her into eating more than she needs. Your baby is the only person who knows how much is enough.

'Remembering not to battle about food was harder as Joshua got older. I had to remember not to bully him and remind myself that he's good at self-regulating and he'll only eat what he wants, so trying to persuade him to eat more never works.'

Sue, mother of Joshua, 3 years

Knowing when she's finished eating

Babies have their own ways of telling their parents they've finished eating and you'll soon learn to interpret your baby's signals. She may look bored, begin playing with her bib or a squashed bit of food, or start wriggling to get down. Dropped food can be a useful sign; young babies drop food by accident but once they have learned to do this on purpose (usually at around nine or ten months), repeated dropping of food generally means that they have lost interest in the meal. Some babies simply push food away from them or make sweeping movements across their tray or the table. If you're not sure what your baby is trying to tell you, offer her a little more (perhaps a different taste) and see how she responds.

'Mabel is an incredibly efficient communicator at mealtimes. Now, when she finishes something, she hands it to me and shakes her head; she'll only start dropping things when we haven't been listening properly. Yesterday she had some falafel she didn't want, so she handed it to me and shook her head.

*But her dad hadn't noticed this, saw no falafel on her plate, and put some
on. She just dumped it straight on the floor, which is totally understandable.'*

Rae, mother of Mabel, 1 year

Snacks and Food on the Move

Until she is at least nine months old, your baby's main between-meal 'snack'
should normally be a milk feed. Once her appetite for other foods really kicks in
(which may not be much before she's a year, or even later), making sure you have
a healthy snack with you when you are out and about will mean you can avoid
buying highly processed foods and sweets to fill a hunger gap.

Snacks are an important part of a child's diet, so think of them as mini meals
rather than as 'extras'. If the snack is nutritious, it doesn't matter if it 'spoils her
appetite' for the next meal. Young children need to eat little and often.

Simple snack ideas

Snacks are really just foods that you can give to your child quickly and easily, whenever
they are needed. Healthy baked snacks such as home-made muffins, scones and
flapjacks are ideal to make in batches and have ready, but there are plenty of foods
that will make perfect snacks that you
may already have in the house:

• Fruit, served whole or as slices
• A handful of dry cereal (low-sugar,
  low-salt variety)
• Oat cakes, rice cakes, toast or bread
  with spread
• A piece of cheese
• Strips of cooked meat or a chicken
  drumstick
• Leftover cooked vegetables (such as
  baby corn, mangetout, green beans, or
  sticks of carrot or courgette)
• Leftovers such as slices of frittata (see
  page 126), home-made pizza (see pages
  133–4), or portions of cold pasta dishes

What to Expect with BLW

Although some things will be the same however you introduce solids to your baby, many aspects of baby-led weaning are quite different from conventional weaning. Here are some things you can expect over the first few months.

Mess!

There's no denying that baby-led weaning can be very messy indeed at the beginning – but the messy phase tends to be short. In the meantime, a clean plastic mat under your baby's chair will protect the floor and allow pieces of food to be safely handed back.

Try to avoid the temptation to wipe your baby's face or hands while she's handling food; it will be annoying for her, and interrupt her concentration and fun. Saving bath time until after dinner is a good idea too.

If you are eating at someone else's house you can take your splash mat, or an old newspaper, with you. You could also take along some non-runny food for your baby, so you'll have something else to offer if the meal looks as though it could be very messy.

Overall, it's important to allow your baby to explore food freely as much as possible both for learning and enjoyment – even if she does make a bit of a mess.

Longer mealtimes

Be prepared to allow your baby plenty of time to learn new skills and to find out about food. Chewing can be a slow business at first but learning to chew effectively is essential for good digestion and to minimise the chance of choking. Hurrying your baby – or trying to 'help' her – will distract her and may delay her progress.

Changing poo

When your baby starts eating solid foods, her poo will change. In fact, the best way of knowing whether your baby is actually swallowing any food in the early days is by what you see in her nappy. If she has managed to swallow some food, her poo will contain 'bits'. Some may look almost the same as when they went in; this is normal and simply reflects her developing chewing skills. Over the next few months, as she begins to eat more and to chew more effectively, you'll notice her poo will become darker, smellier and more solid.

> *'Felix loves cooked beetroot (with no vinegar), and he'll eat loads. But it goes straight through him and makes his poo dark red or purple!'*
>
> Tom, father of Felix, 2 years

Getting frustrated

Sometimes babies go through a phase of appearing frustrated with food. This is similar to the frustration that sometimes happens with a new toy; it isn't caused by your baby needing (and not being able to eat) the food she's trying to get to her mouth, it's simply impatience at skills that are developing more slowly than she would like. So there's no need to spoon feed her or put the food in her mouth for her; the frustration won't last long if she's allowed to work it out for herself.

However, before you decide that your baby is just a bit frustrated, check the following:

- Is she tired or hungry? Babies can change their feeding and sleeping patterns without warning, so today may not be the same as yesterday.
- Is she comfortable and able to reach the food easily? She may need a bit of extra support so she can lean forward.
- Are the pieces of food the right size and shape for her to grasp? Or, if she is older and is finding a new skill difficult (such as picking up peas), does she have some pieces of food that she can easily manage alongside the tricky ones?

- Would she prefer to sit on your lap for a few meals, to help her to feel more confident?

Food choices

Babies and small children occasionally want to eat nothing but one particular food, sometimes for several days at a time. These unpredictable food 'fads' are quite normal. Just continue to offer your baby varied, healthy meals and let her choose from them what she wants to eat – even if her diet doesn't seem particularly well balanced on the day, it will probably even out over the course of a week or so.

BLW basics
- Offer food at times when your baby isn't tired or hungry.
- Allow your baby to explore food and play with it.
- Start by offering foods that are easy to pick up – preferably the same as those you are eating.
- Offer a variety of foods throughout the week, with different tastes and textures, avoiding foods that aren't nutritious.
- Don't expect her to eat very much for the first few months. Her appetite for solid food will probably start to increase anytime from around nine months to a year.
- Carry on offering breast or formula feeds. Expect your baby's milk-feeding pattern to change only very gradually as she starts to eat more.
- Don't hurry your baby or distract her while she is handling food, or try to persuade her to eat more than she wants.
- Offer your baby water with her meals, in case she is thirsty.

Keeping mealtimes safe
- Make sure your baby is sitting upright to eat, not leaning back or slumping.
- Keep whole nuts out of your baby's reach.
- Offer larger fruits, such as apples, whole or cut into big pieces; cut small fruits such as grapes and cherries in half and remove any stones or pips.
- Remove skins from sausages, and gristle and small bones from meat and fish.
- Don't let anyone except your baby put food into her mouth – including 'helpful' older children.
- Explain how baby-led weaning works to anyone caring for your baby.
- NEVER leave your baby alone with food.

If your baby rejects a particular food it doesn't necessarily mean she doesn't like it. It probably means she doesn't want or need that food at that time. If it's something you serve regularly, carry on offering it – she'll probably change her mind in a few days.

Gagging

Don't be surprised if your baby gags occasionally when she starts feeding herself with solid foods. This is quite normal (see pages 15–16) and is not the same as choking – it's just a way of pushing forward food that needs a bit more chewing. For some babies, gagging leads to a small vomit. However, although it can be a bit disconcerting to watch, it doesn't seem to bother them – and it happens less and less often as they learn to control food in their mouths more effectively.

If your baby starts to gag, make sure she is sitting upright or leaning slightly forward, so that the food she's trying to move can fall out of her mouth, rather than going back towards her throat. Slapping her on the back won't help her (and may make her more likely to choke), so try to stay calm while she deals with it, and smile at her once she's sorted it out.

'Every time Amy gagged I was ready to jump up and flip her over but once I got used to letting her have that extra few seconds she'd deal with it and be halfway through the next mouthful of food by the time I'd recovered!'

Emily, mother of Amy, 6 months

Gradual progress

Each baby is different, and baby-led weaning allows them to develop their eating skills at their own unique pace, rather than in clear 'stages' (as with conventional weaning). As with any new skill your baby learns, it will probably be two steps forward and one step back, for example, she may start using cutlery for a couple of weeks and then go back to using her fingers for a month or two. All of this is normal. In fact, as your baby progresses with baby-led weaning, it's likely that her abilities will take you by surprise as she gradually becomes more and more accomplished at mealtimes.

Chapter Four

WHAT TO EAT

Baby-led weaning is all about sharing healthy family food with your baby; most food that is good for you is good for your baby, too. So as long as you offer a varied, balanced diet that is made up mainly of fresh and healthy ingredients, and avoid the few foods babies shouldn't have, you won't go far wrong – and your baby will be well on the way to developing a taste for nutritious meals that will help him to make sensible food choices when he is older.

A Healthy Diet

A healthy diet for the whole family is one that provides all the necessary nutrients in roughly the right proportions, and gives you all plenty of energy. In the first few months of solids there's no need to worry about balancing the different types of food for your baby because he is still just exploring; his milk feeds (breast milk or formula) contain all the nutrients he needs. And, unless there are allergies in the family, there's no need to introduce foods one at a time (as parents used to be advised to do) because by six months babies' digestive and immune systems can cope with a wide variety of foods. If your baby shares healthy meals with you, as soon as he does begin to need extra nutrients they will be readily available for him.

There are four main food groups: fruit and vegetables, starchy foods, protein-rich foods and calcium-rich foods, plus a fifth, smaller group – fats. Adults (and older children) should aim to have plenty of starchy foods, with smaller amounts of protein foods, calcium-rich foods, and a small amount of fat. Babies' needs are slightly different (see pages 36–7), although the 'five-a-day' rule for fruit and vegetables, along with the advice to eat fish at least twice a week, is a good guide for both babies and adults.

Food groups

Fruit and vegetables provide important vitamins and minerals. Try to offer as many differently coloured fruit and vegetables as you can – they all provide different nutrients.

Starchy foods provide energy, and many also contain protein, as well as some important vitamins and minerals. Examples are wheat, rice, oats and other grains (and foods made from them, such as bread and pasta), as well as starchy vegetables such as potatoes and yams.

Protein-rich foods are vital for growth. Meat, fish, eggs and cheese are all full of protein and are excellent foods for babies. Tofu and quinoa are the highest plant sources of protein, while pulses (such as beans, chickpeas and lentils) and nuts are also protein-rich.

Calcium-rich foods include dairy foods, such as milk, cheese and yoghurt, tofu, sesame seeds (for example as hummus), almonds, and canned fish with soft, edible bones, such as sardines.

Fats provide energy in a concentrated form. Some fats are important for the healthy functioning and development of the brain. They are found in good quantities in fish (especially oily fish), avocados, nuts and seeds. Fats are also plentiful in meat, eggs and dairy foods. Adults shouldn't have too many saturated fats (mainly animal fats, from meat, cheese and butter) and the whole family should avoid trans-fats, or fats that have been hydrogenated (as contained in some margarines, and normally used in shop-bought pies, biscuits and cakes).

'When Kyle was eight or nine months he loved dark green vegetables like Brussels sprouts – in fact anything with lots of vitamin C he seemed to go for first.'
Linda, mother of Kyle, 16 months

Extra needs for babies

Babies and young children need more fat and calcium than adults. Breast milk and infant formula contain plenty of these important nutrients, but as babies gradually start to have less breast milk or formula (usually from about nine months onwards), they need to get fat and calcium from the rest of their diet in order to grow and develop healthily. So although a low-fat diet may be better for their parents and older siblings, children under two years old, who aren't relying on milk feeds, should have full-fat dairy foods (milk, yoghurt, butter and cheese) to ensure that they get all the nutrients and energy they require. Oily fish with edible bones are a good source of both fat and calcium, as are nut butters, almonds and sesame seeds.

Iron and zinc are the first nutrients that babies start to need in addition to those provided by breast milk. Most babies are born with stores of these minerals to last them well beyond six months, but it's a good idea to offer foods that contain them early on, so that your baby can help himself to them as soon as he needs them. Most foods that are rich in iron are also good sources of zinc. Slow-cooked meat (especially beef) is the best source, and fish and eggs also provide plenty. Tofu, pulses and dark green leafy vegetables contain good amounts of iron (and zinc) – although it's not as easily absorbed as it is from animal sources. In the UK, all bread, wheat flour and many breakfast cereals are fortified with iron. Eating foods that contain vitamin C (most vegetables and fruit) at the same meal as iron-rich foods helps to maximise iron absorption – even a squeeze of lemon juice makes a difference. (See page 44 for specific information on iron for vegetarians.)

From about eight or nine months onwards, when your baby is eating more and may be beginning to take less milk, making sure you offer him something from each of the main food groups every day, along with his milk feeds, will provide him with a good range of nutrients. Don't worry if he chooses not to eat some of each – he will balance out his diet over the course of a few days, provided he is allowed to choose freely.

The importance of variety

The best way to provide a good range of nutrients for your baby is to offer a truly varied diet each week. Having a variety of foods will also provide different tastes and textures for him to learn to manage – and the more naturally colourful the food is, the better the range of vitamins and minerals it is likely to contain.

It's a good idea to have a look at your own diet to see if you are buying the same foods (however healthy) week after week. If you are, try some new foods – even changing the cuts of meat or the type of bread you normally buy can provide you with a different selection of nutrients. Swapping wheat-based meals for other grains, such as oats or millet, now and then will add extra vitamins and minerals, and varying the fruit and vegetables you buy, and including some fresh herbs, will also help to ensure a wide range of nutrients for the whole family. (Meal planning can help with this, see page 47.)

'Because Charlotte eats with us she has tasted and loves curry, chilli, Japanese, Italian, Caribbean and Thai – in fact the more flavour the better. The only three things she hates with a passion are banana, carrot and cheese. We have no battles and mealtimes are fun – eating out is brilliant.'

Samantha, mother of Charlotte, 1 year

Foods to Avoid

Although your baby can share most of the food you
eat, you need to take care with some ingredients,
which are bad for babies. These are discussed below,
starting with the most important – salt.

Salt

A baby's immature kidneys can't cope with too
much salt and it can make them very ill, so it's
important to avoid it as much as possible. A
high-salt diet early on may also make babies more
prone to high blood pressure later in life.

Salt shouldn't be added to any food that is going
to be offered to your baby. If you are used to adding
salt to your cooking at home, you'll probably find
cooking with lemon, herbs and spices can satisfy
your need for a 'fuller' flavour – or you can add salt
to your own food at the table.

However, while it's relatively easy to avoid salt when you're cooking from scratch,
most (around 80 per cent) of the salt we eat is 'hidden' in processed foods as a
flavour enhancer and preservative, so it's important to know what to look out for
when you are buying food. The worst culprits are ready-made gravies, stocks and
sauces, tinned foods and ready-meals.

Checking labels will help you to choose healthier options – some types and brands
of bread, croissants and pastries (especially those baked in-store or served in cafés
and restaurants) contain much more salt than others that look the same. Even some
bottled mineral waters have very high salt levels. Baked beans, cheese and ham can
vary enormously, too, depending on the brand. Once you've worked out which
brand has the least salt you can just buy that one again next time, so you don't have
to read the labels on every shopping trip.

However, labels can be confusing because manufacturers are required to list how
much sodium (or 'Na') the food contains, rather than how much salt. This can make
a product appear less salty than it really is – to work out the salt content you need to
multiply the sodium content by 2.5. The lists opposite and overleaf will help you
spot the foods that are good and bad for your baby, in terms of salt, and the grid
opposite shows the recommended daily salt limit for babies and toddlers.

Total daily salt (sodium) limits, as recommended by the UK Department of Health		
Child's age	**Daily salt limit**	**Equivalent in sodium**
6–12 months	1g	0.4g (400mg)
1–2 years	2g	0.8g (800mg)

NB: The recommended daily salt limit for adults is 6g.

If the food has more than 1.5g salt per 100g it is classed as very salty, so your baby shouldn't have any at all or only the tiniest amount. (Some foods have as much as 4g of salt per 100g – or even more. Even a small amount of one of these foods could exceed your baby's recommended daily salt limit.) It's all too easy to give babies more salt than they should have, so it really is worth taking the time to check.

At a glance – salty foods

The following foods are fairly salty but they are okay for babies to have in small quantities occasionally. Try not to offer your baby more than one food from this list in any one day:

- Breakfast cereals with high salt/sugar levels (choose the lowest you can find)
- Hard cheeses, such as Cheddar, and processed varieties such as Edam
- Sausages, especially pepperoni, chorizo and salami-type sausages
- Ham and bacon
- Smoked or salted fish, such as kippers and anchovies
- Foods preserved in brine, such as tuna and olives (choose those preserved in oil or spring water instead)
- Baked beans (choose low-salt and low-sugar varieties, preferably organic)
- Yeast extract (e.g. Marmite)
- Ready-to-cook pizza
- In-store bakery products such as ciabatta, pastries and cheese straws

39

The following foods are very salty and are not suitable for babies:
- Crisps, tortilla chips and other salty snacks
- Ready-made savoury pies
- Many ready-meals
- Most take-away foods and 'fast foods', such as burgers, pizzas, etc.
- Some ready-made sauces for pasta or curry
- Most ready-made gravies and stocks, including granules and cubes (choose lower-salt versions)
- Sauces such as ketchup, brown sauce, barbecue sauce and soy sauce
- Tinned or packet (dried) soups
- Processed cheese foods, such as 'Dunkers' and 'Cheese Strings'

Balancing salt

When you're planning meals, it's worth bearing in mind the amount of something salty your baby is likely to eat. A meal that consists only of ham, cheese and salty bread could well put a strain on his kidneys, but one that includes a small amount of ham alongside plenty of vegetables and fruit is unlikely to cause him any harm. If you are eating at a restaurant or at a relative's house, where the food could contain a lot of salt, try to make sure that your child is offered the most nutritious parts of the meal with as little gravy or sauce as possible. If he does have something very salty, make sure he can drink as much water (or breast milk) as he needs, both with the meal and later, and that his other meals that day are low in salt.

'We really don't make anything different for Ed. The first time round we had to get used to eating food without salt, but now we are used to it there isn't anything I wouldn't offer him – I just don't think about it now. We have healthy food – he has what we have.'

Ria, mother of Jake, 2 years, and Ed, 10 months

Other Foods to Avoid

There are several other foods that babies shouldn't be offered, besides salt. Some, such as raw shellfish or undercooked eggs, carry a risk of food poisoning or infection; some can cause harm such as tooth decay; while others simply don't contain enough nutrients.

Sugar

Sugar provides only 'empty calories' – it doesn't have any essential nutrients. It also contributes to tooth decay. If you can avoid giving your child a sugary diet in the early years, he is less likely to crave very sweet things as he gets older. Children will only expect a sweet dessert at mealtimes if they usually have one (and if they do, they will quickly learn to save some room for their dessert by eating less of their main course). Some foods aimed at children, such as cereals or flavoured yoghurts, can contain a lot of sugar – every 5g of sugar mentioned on the label is about a teaspoonful of sugar. Sucrose, dextrose, fruit syrup and glucose are all forms of sugar, too.

Sweet dishes that include a small amount of sugar are okay to offer your baby occasionally, especially if they're otherwise nutritious (apple crumble or fruit cake, for example). Ingredients such as dried or fresh fruits can often be used as a sweetener, with no need for any extra sugar at all. And adding sweet spices, such as cinnamon, to dessert and cake recipes helps to enhance their overall sweetness.

Don't be tempted to use an artificial sweetener to replace real sugar in your recipes, or to buy foods that are low in sugar but contain artificial sweeteners (such as aspartame) – they carry their own health risks, and they won't stop your child developing a liking for very sweet food.

Sweets contain no useful nutrients and can fill babies' tummies, leaving little room for more nutritious foods. They are also likely to contain additives (see below).

Additives

Additives such as monosodium glutamate and e-numbers, which are usually artificial preservatives, flavours and sweeteners, should be avoided as much as possible – they don't contain any nutrients and may even be harmful (which is why they are not allowed in commercial baby foods). Government research suggests the following, generally found in sweets or desserts, may be linked to hyperactivity in children, so should be avoided: Tartrazine (E102), Quinoline yellow (E104), Sunset yellow (E110), Carmoisine (E122), Ponceau 4R (E124), Allura red (E129) and Sodium benzoate (E211).

Ready-meals and junk foods

Ready-meals – even those labelled as 'low fat' – and junk foods, such as cheap burgers, pizzas and pies, are completely unsuitable for babies. In general, these foods are very highly processed and contain a great deal of salt, sugar, artificial additives and hydrogenated fats, with very few nutrients.

Honey

Babies shouldn't have honey until they are over one year old because it can be the source of an infection called botulism.

Certain types of fish

Shark, swordfish and marlin should be avoided because they contain potentially high levels of mercury, which can affect the development of the nervous system. Raw shellfish carry a high risk of food poisoning – they are safe only if thoroughly cooked. Although oily fish (such as salmon, trout, mackerel, herring, sardines and fresh tuna) is very nutritious, girls and women of childbearing age shouldn't eat it more than twice a week because of the possible build-up of pollutants (boys, men and older women can have up to four portions per week). Canned tuna doesn't contain the same toxins as fresh tuna or other oily fish, so it can be eaten more often.

Undercooked eggs

Eggs often contain salmonella, which can make a baby very ill. Cooking destroys the bug so, provided they are thoroughly cooked so that the yolk is firm, eggs can form part of your baby's diet. (The old advice, to avoid egg whites, is not relevant for babies over six months, as babies this age are better able to tolerate them.) Mayonnaise, shop-bought ice cream that is labelled 'home-made', and some desserts, such as chocolate mousse or tiramisu, usually contain raw eggs, so shouldn't be given to babies.

Bran and high-fibre foods

Raw bran and high-fibre cereals (such as All-bran and some muesli) can interfere with the absorption of iron and other essential nutrients, so they are not good for babies. They are also very filling and don't contain enough calories or nutrients. If you are offering wholegrain cereals (such as brown rice and pasta) make sure your baby has a choice of some starchy foods that contain less fibre as well.

Hydrogenated fats

Hydrogenated fats, also known as trans-fatty acids, are thought to interfere with the beneficial actions of healthy fats. They are found in many processed foods, such as biscuits, pies, crisps, ready-meals and in some margarines and lard. Most healthy foods don't contain them.

Drinks to Avoid

The only drinks babies really need are water and breast milk (which can be a thirst-quenching drink as well as a food). Other drinks will tend to fill your baby up, leaving no room for more nutritious food or milk feeds.

Caffeinated drinks, such as coffee, tea and cola, can make babies irritable; tea also interferes with iron absorption. Fizzy or fruit-flavoured drinks are very sugary and acidic (so not good for teeth) and many contain additives. Pure fruit juice is okay in small quantities but it should be diluted one part juice to ten parts water.

Cows' milk shouldn't be given as a drink to babies under one year old because it fills them up with the wrong balance of nutrients. The same applies to goats' and sheep's milks. It's okay, though, to use these milks in cooking or – provided they are pasteurised – with breakfast cereals, for babies of six months and older.

Allergies

Although babies over six months are able to tolerate a wider range of foods than younger babies, if there is a history of food allergies in your family it's a good idea to introduce solid foods carefully. Allowing three days between foods that may be likely

Common allergens
Foods you may wish to introduce carefully if there are allergies in the family:

- Cows' milk (also goats' and sheep's milk)
- Eggs
- Peanuts (which aren't true nuts but are related to pulses)
- Wheat (and other grains that contain gluten)
- Soya beans
- Fish
- Shellfish
- Nuts
- Seeds (especially sesame)
- Citrus fruits
- Tomatoes
- Strawberries

to cause a problem will give you time to spot a reaction (such as itchy skin or a rash, diarrhoea, vomiting, tummy pain, swollen lips, sore eyes or wheezing). Breastfeeding for as long as possible will help to reduce the risk of allergies, and is especially protective while new foods are being introduced. It's also important to have a truly varied diet, so that your baby doesn't eat too much of any one food. If you suspect a food allergy or intolerance, talk to your doctor or health visitor.

'Polly was spoon fed and had allergies, and has always been a bit picky. But, now she sees her baby sister eating lots of new things, she'll try them. Evie is encouraging her to be more adventurous.'

Anisa, mother of Polly, 3 years, and Evie, 8 months

Vegetarian Diets

If you are planning to bring your baby up as a vegetarian you'll need to make sure he has plenty of iron and protein from non-meat sources. Fish (if you eat it), eggs, tofu, and pulses, such as lentils, beans, chickpeas and split peas, are good sources of both protein and iron. Dried fruit, such as apricots and figs, and (low-sugar, low-salt) fortified cereals can also be a useful source of iron. The absorption of iron is helped by vitamin C, so it's a good idea to include foods that are high in vitamin C, such as red berries, tomatoes and citrus fruits, with meals, or to offer dilute, freshly squeezed fruit juice as a drink.

Vegan diets are generally considered to be too low in important fats, B vitamins, zinc, calcium and some amino acids (as well as iron) to be safe for babies and so supplements are almost always needed. Breastfeeding for at least two years, if possible, will help to ensure good nutrition but we recommend you talk to a nutritionist or dietitian if you want your baby to have a vegan diet.

Chapter Five
MAKING MEALTIMES SIMPLE

Baby-led weaning is an easy way to feed your baby, but organising family mealtimes can still be tricky for busy parents. Here are some ideas to make it a little easier.

Cooking with a Baby

Even if you are an experienced cook, preparing a meal when you have a baby or toddler can present new challenges – especially if you have gone back to work. Babies' patterns are unpredictable and most babies will need some attention in less time than it takes to cook the average meal. So you will probably need to take advantage of small chunks of baby-free time whenever you can – and to find creative ways of doing things when you can't.

Some babies are quite happy to sit for short periods in a bouncy chair or to lie on a mat with their toys while their mum or dad cooks, provided they can see them. An older baby may be content to sit in her highchair with some snacks and watch you. A sling can be really useful – preferably one that you can wear on your back or side as well as your front, so that your baby can snuggle up to you safely, away from any hot pans, oven doors and sharp knives. Most babies will settle in a sling for long periods of time, and may even fall asleep there.

Getting family meals on the table is easier if you can break down your cooking tasks into stages and work out what can be done when. For example, you may be able to make your pasta sauce ahead of time, or wash and peel your vegetables and put them in the fridge early in the day, to be cut up later for an evening meal.

'Arthur loves to watch me cook. He'll sit in his highchair with a rice cake and I'll talk about all the food as I'm preparing it and show him what I'm doing – he's quite happy.'

Caroline, mother of Arthur, 11 months

Batch Cooking and Freezing

Cooking in bulk – or batch cooking – is a great way to save time (and money) and is invaluable when you are especially busy or if you return to work after maternity leave. Many dishes and sauces can be frozen successfully, enabling you to thaw out either a complete meal or one that's already half-made.

Some parents buy in bulk and spend a couple of hours cooking large amounts and freezing it in smaller portions. Others simply cook twice as much as they need when they're making something like lasagne, and freeze half. Even preparing and freezing small portions of things such as chopped onions or grated cheese can make a difference.

Foods suitable for preparing in advance

- Main dishes, such as lasagne, meatballs, patties, chilli con carne, stew and meat loaf.
- Stocks, soups and sauces, including pasta sauces and home-made gravy.
- Cooked minced meat with onions (to use for dishes such as shepherd's pie).
- Pre-prepared vegetables (especially anything fiddly to chop with a baby on your hip, such as onions), fruit and grated cheese.
- Uncooked pastry and dough, bread, some cakes, muffins, scones, pancakes.
- Spare ingredients, such as tomato purée and lemon juice (freeze in ice cube trays).

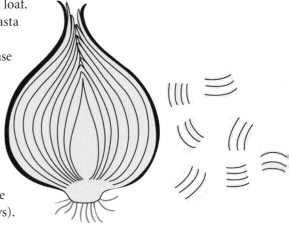

Tips for freezing home-cooked food

- Cooked food should be allowed to cool at room temperature, then transferred into suitable airtight containers and frozen as soon as possible.
- Dividing food into small or individual portions before freezing helps it to freeze (and defrost) more quickly. (Sauce can be divided into portions in a muffin tin (or yoghurt pots); once frozen, put them into a single container for storage.)
- Food expands when frozen so containers should be left around a third empty.
- It can be hard to identify frozen food, so remember to label containers with the contents and date.
- Freezers should be set at -18°C (0°F) or below. If you are planning to freeze a lot of food in one go, set your freezer temperature to -23°C (-9°F) at least 24 hours beforehand.
- The maximum storage time for most frozen home-cooked food is around two to three months (to retain nutrients, taste and appearance).
- The majority of food is best defrosted slowly in the fridge before it is reheated. If you defrost food in a microwave, reheat it straight away.
- Defrosted meals should be eaten within 24 hours of removing from the freezer.
- Defrosted foods should be reheated thoroughly. Check that the food is steaming hot in the middle before serving (but let it cool before offering it to your baby).
- Any leftovers should be thrown away – don't re-freeze or reheat anything twice.

Meal Planning

Planning ahead can make organising mealtimes, food shopping – and batch cooking – much easier. It's also a useful way to make sure you are offering your baby a variety of tastes and textures. Many families get into a pattern of eating the same few favourite dishes each week without really realising it – planning can help you avoid this.

Writing down an outline of your main meals for a two-week period will help you to see at a glance whether there's a good balance of main ingredients, and to spot 'samey' meals. If you notice any foods, textures or tastes that are missing, you can choose some new recipes or ingredients to fill the gaps.

Food Safety

Kitchens can be a breeding ground for the bacteria that cause food poisoning, so it's important to follow some basic rules to keep you and your family safe.

Routine food hygiene

Wash your hands thoroughly with soap and warm water and dry them before handling food, between the handling of raw and ready-to-eat foods, after touching the rubbish bin, after handling cleaning materials, after changing your baby's nappy and after touching pets, their bedding or food bowls. Everyone in the family should wash their hands before eating (wash your baby's hands before offering him food).

Kitchen surfaces should be cleaned before and after you prepare food. Chopping boards and knives should always be washed thoroughly after use but you need to be extra careful after cutting up raw meat or fish. Having a separate chopping board for raw fish and meat will help to prevent the spread of harmful bacteria.

Storing and cooking food

Perishable food should be kept in the fridge, which should be set at between 1–5°C (34–41°F). Adding warm foods or leaving the door open will raise the temperature, so make sure food has cooled down fully before putting it in the fridge and try not to open the door more than necessary. Raw meat and fish should be covered, on a plate or in a bag (especially when defrosting), and kept on the lowest shelf, to prevent any juices touching or dripping on to other foods. Foods that go off quickly should be stored on the shelves rather than in the fridge door (which is the least cold part of the fridge).

Always cook food thoroughly, paying attention to cooking times and temperatures given in recipes. Take care with foods that need special preparation, such as some dried beans (see page 51), and consider buying fridge and meat thermometers.

Leftovers should be cooled, then put into the fridge as soon as possible, especially any dishes that contain meat, chicken, fish, seafood, eggs or rice. Rice that is not to be eaten straight away should be cooled, by washing it with cold water, then refrigerated immediately. This is because the spores of some food-poisoning bugs multiply in rice (and other grains) at room temperature and cannot be killed, even if the food is thoroughly reheated. All cooked foods and leftovers should be kept at the top of the fridge and eaten within two days.

Finally, follow storage instructions given on food packages, check 'best before' dates regularly, and don't give your baby foods that are past their 'use by' date.

Part Two
The Recipes

These recipes are all baby-led weaning favourites. They are easy to make, tasty and nutritious, and will provide a range of tastes and textures for your baby to explore and for everyone to enjoy. Don't be afraid to experiment with the recipes – they are not set in stone. Most of them are fairly simple and the ingredients or amounts (or even methods) can often be changed or adapted. We've made some suggestions, but really it's up to you. Enjoy!

GETTING STARTED

Some Notes on Ingredients

- Try to use **fresh ingredients** as far as possible, and, when you can, go for produce that is seasonal, locally grown and organic. The flavour of these foods is often better, and with organic foods you can guarantee that your baby won't be exposed to the chemicals commonly used in food production.
- Where a recipe includes **milk**, this means full-fat cow's milk, unless otherwise stated. Most of the recipes should also work with other animal milks or with rice or soya milks, but we can't guarantee this.
- **Flour** is assumed to be wheat flour, unless otherwise stated. Generally, it is considered safe for babies over six months to eat wheat, but it may be an ingredient you are keen to avoid if you have intolerances in the family (see page 43–4). Spelt flour is made from a type of wheat that is easier to digest than ordinary wheat. Or you may prefer to use a gluten-free flour, such as buckwheat (not wheat, despite the name), rice, maize or potato flour. Gluten-free flours are generally okay for cooking, although they may result in a slightly different texture and won't work in recipes that use yeast.
- Aim to use unsalted **butter** wherever possible, because it's better for babies than butter containing salt. If you would rather not use dairy products, you can use oil, or a vegetable-based margarine (one that is free from hydrogenated oils or trans-fats).
- When the recipe refers simply to **cheese**, you can use any hard cheese, such as Cheddar, Red Leicester, Monterey Jack, Emmenthal or Sbrinz. These will all work in recipes where the cheese is grated and needs to melt. Non-melting cheeses, such as halloumi, feta, paneer and ricotta, won't work in these recipes.
- Where a recipe calls for **cream cheese**, this means a fresh white cream cheese, such as mascarpone or Philadelphia, not a cheese spread like Dairylea.
- The weights in the recipes are for dried **pasta and noodles**, rather than fresh (which weigh more). Most pasta is wheat-based and fresh pasta usually contains egg, so if you are trying to avoid these foods you will need to use an alternative, such as rice noodles or corn pasta.
- Dried **herbs** are more concentrated than fresh; as a general rule 1 tsp of dried herbs is equivalent to 3 tsp (1 tbsp) of fresh herbs. (To chop fresh herbs easily, use a pair of sharp scissors, and chop over a bowl or in a cup.)

- **Ginger** means root ginger. If the root is thick, use less than the recipe says.
- For **lemon, lime or orange zest**, use a fine grater to take off the extreme outside, or coloured part, of the rind of the fruit – the whitish pith can be very bitter.
- Where a recipe calls for **breadcrumbs** – unless it says fresh – it means stale or dried. To make breadcrumbs, grate day-old bread (dry it in the oven first if necessary).
- Fresh and dried **chillies** (flakes and powder) vary in potency so start by using a little until you find out how hot your baby likes his food. The 'heat' from raw chilli pepper can linger for hours so be careful not to touch your baby's hands, eyes, nose or mouth, or to change his nappy, before you've washed your hands thoroughly.
- Where a recipe uses tinned **pulses** (for example, chickpeas or red kidney beans), dried versions can be used instead but may need pre-soaking and/or pre-cooking (see chart below). Although you can use different types of pulse in most dishes, you may need to adjust the recipe preparation time. Take care if using red kidney beans or soya beans – they can be harmful if they are not soaked and cooked for long enough (tinned varieties are ready to eat). Lentils, split peas, black-eye beans and mung beans don't need any pre-soaking or pre-cooking.

Soaking and cooking times for pulses

	Pre-soaking time	*Pre-cooking time*	*Cooking time to soften*
Chickpeas, borlotti beans, butter beans, cannellini beans, black beans, fava beans, flageolet beans, lima beans, pinto beans, azuki beans	Up to 12 hours	No pre-cooking needed but boiling them for 10 minutes will cut down the cooking time	Up to 1 hour
Red kidney beans	Up to 12 hours	10 minutes, boiling rapidly	45–60 minutes
Soya beans	Up to 12 hours	1 hour, boiling rapidly	2–3 hours

To pre-soak: Put the dried pulses into a large pan or bowl, pour in enough cold water to treble their volume, cover and leave for the required time. Drain and rinse.
To pre-cook: Put the pre-soaked pulses into a pan of fresh water, bring them to the boil and boil rapidly (not simmering) for the required time. Drain and rinse.

Technical Stuff

Ovens

The recipes give instructions for cooking using a standard hob or oven, although some recipes include an alternative method for microwaves. However, if you want to use a microwave for part of a recipe, such as pre-cooking vegetables or melting butter, that's fine.

Most ovens take at least 15 minutes to heat up and it's usually best to wait until the oven is at the required temperature before putting the food in. Grills also need to be pre-heated.

Unless they are fan-assisted, all ovens tend to be hotter at the top, affecting how fast food cooks (and whether or not it gets burnt!); you can cook two dishes that require slightly different temperatures in the oven at the same time by putting them on different shelves.

Temperatures given in recipes are always a guide only, so you will need to experiment with your own oven to get a feel for whether you need to adjust the temperatures up or down. If you have a fan-assisted oven you may find that the food cooks better at slightly lower temperatures than those given in most recipes so you will need to adjust your timings accordingly.

Basic cooking terms

- To **sift** flour pass it through a fine sieve, shaking gently. This adds air and removes lumps. If using wholemeal flour, add the bran left in the sieve to the sifted flour.
- To **simmer** a dish in a pan, the liquid should be just bubbling occasionally; when **boiling**, the liquid should be bubbling continuously.
- **Parboiling** means boiling for part of the time needed to fully cook the food.
- **Blanching** means putting food very briefly into boiling water. (This is all the cooking needed for some vegetables – spinach for example.) Some recipes suggest blanching tomatoes to loosen the skin so they can be peeled more easily.
- **Sautéing** is frying food quickly in hot oil in a shallow pan.

Weights and measures

Many recipes online or in American (or old) cookery books, use cups or ounces for measuring ingredients, rather than grams and millilitres. The tables below and overleaf give the approximate equivalents for the most commonly used units.

- When measuring with cups and spoons the food should be level with the sides of the spoon or cup, i.e. flat, not heaped or packed down.
- It's best not to mix metric and imperial measurements in one recipe – stick to a single type of measurement for the best result. (That way, you might end up with a slightly smaller cake, for example, but at least the ingredients will be in the right proportions, so the cake will 'work'.)

METRIC WEIGHT	IMPERIAL WEIGHT	AMERICAN CUP		
		Powdery foods, e.g. flour	Sugars and fats	Dense foods, e.g. syrup
25g	1oz		¼ cup	
50g	1¾oz			
100g	3½oz		½ cup	
150g	5½oz	1 cup		½ cup
200g	7oz		1 cup	
250g	9oz			
300g	10½oz	2 cups	1½ cups	
350g	12½oz			1 cup
400g	14oz		2 cups	
500g	1lb 2oz	3 cups		
1kg	2lb 3oz			

g = gram
kg = kilogram
oz = ounce
lb = pound
1kg = 1000g
1lb = 16oz (455g)

Metric volume	Imperial volume (UK)	American spoon/cup
5ml	1 tsp	1 tsp
15ml	1 tbsp	1 tbsp
25ml	1fl oz	⅛ cup
50ml	2fl oz	¼ cup
100ml	3½fl oz	½ cup
150ml	5fl oz (¼ pint)	
200ml	7fl oz	
250ml	9fl oz	1 cup
300ml	11fl oz (½ pint)	1¼ cups
350ml	12fl oz	
400ml	14fl oz	
450ml	16fl oz	2 cups
500ml	17½fl oz	
550ml	20fl oz (1 pint)	
1 litre	1¾ pints	1 quart

ml = millilitre
fl oz = fluid ounce

tsp = teaspoon
tbsp = tablespoon

1 litre = 1000ml
1 pint = 20fl oz (568ml)

BREAKFAST

Don't be surprised if your baby shows no interest in breakfast for the first few months of solid foods; all many babies want first thing in the morning is a cuddle and a milk feed. Once your baby is ready to join in with breakfast, however, there are plenty of ways you can adapt your usual food or try something new.

It's easy for adults to get into a habit of having the same thing for breakfast every day, but it's a good idea to vary what you offer to your baby so that he has the chance to discover different tastes and textures and get a good range of nutrients.

The recipes that follow will give you some ideas for tasty alternatives to your 'usual' breakfast – and many of them will work just as well for lunch or teatime too.

Breakfast Ideas

Here are some tips for really simple breakfasts for your baby.

Fresh fruit

Fresh fruit, served whole or sliced (see pages 25–6) makes a superb breakfast.

Fruit with yoghurt

A note on cereals: *Many breakfast cereals aren't really suitable for babies; those aimed at children are often very salty and/or sugary, and some that are good for adults (high-fibre, bran-based cereals) are not good for babies.*

Fresh, stewed or puréed fruit, served with full-fat natural yoghurt (preferably live) is a simple but delicious breakfast. Your toddler can stir the fruit in while your baby can practise dipping skills or using a spoon, either pre-loaded by you and offered to him or, when he can manage it, loaded himself.

Easy breakfast bix

If the rest of the family has breakfast biscuits (such as Weetabix) the traditional way –
in a bowl with milk on top – you may find this too difficult or messy for your baby
to handle. To make it easier, drip about 2 tsp of milk onto the biscuit, wait for it to
soak in, then add more if it seems to need it. The aim is to make it soft but not
soggy, so it holds together like a soft rusk. He will find this much easier to pick up.

Super-cooked egg

An overcooked fried or poached egg is solid enough for a baby to pick up easily and is a
good way to help him discover the difference between the white and the yolk. Just fry or
poach an egg as normal (using the minimum of oil if frying), but leave it cooking until
the yolk is firm all the way through. Let it cool a bit, then trim off any crispy edges.

Eggy Bread (French Toast)

Eggy bread makes a great breakfast – or your baby may enjoy it cold as a snack.

Serves 1 adult and 1 baby

2 eggs
a little milk (optional – it makes the eggs go further)
4 slices of bread
oil or butter (preferably unsalted) for frying

In a bowl, beat the eggs and add the milk, if using. Dip the bread into the egg mix,
turning as necessary to coat both sides.

Heat the oil or butter in a frying pan and fry the eggy bread on both sides over a
medium to high heat until the egg is thoroughly cooked
and the whole thing is golden brown.

Cut into pieces (finger shapes are usually easiest for
young babies; toddlers may prefer triangles) and serve
immediately, or once cool enough for your baby to handle.

Storage: *Eggy bread is best eaten fresh, but can be frozen and reheated in a microwave. To freeze, allow to cool completely and pack in an airtight container, separating the slices with greaseproof paper.*

Option

• Add a pinch of cinnamon to the beaten egg mix for a
warm, spicy flavour.

Scrambled Eggs

Scrambled eggs make a healthy start to your day – just check your baby's portion is cooked through before offering it.

Serves 1 adult and 1 baby

3 eggs
1 tbsp milk (optional – it gives a softer consistency)
pinch of freshly ground black pepper (optional)
small knob of butter (preferably unsalted)

In a bowl, beat the eggs then add the milk (if using) and black pepper to taste.

Melt the butter in a small saucepan over a gentle heat. Pour in the egg mixture and keep stirring as it thickens. Continue for 5–10 minutes until all the egg has set. (You can also cook scrambled eggs in a bowl in the microwave. Use the High setting and cook for about 1 minute, stirring and checking every 15 seconds.)

Serve immediately, or once cool enough for your baby, with toast, a bagel, an English muffin or a croissant.

Options

- You can add anything you like to the egg mixture provided it will cook (or heat through) in the time it takes the egg to cook. Try a little finely chopped ham, chorizo or salami; some grated cheese; a few thinly sliced mushrooms (tinned or pre-cooked); or some finely chopped onion (this is best softened first by frying gently in the butter before the egg mixture goes in).
- Adding some herbs, such as finely chopped fresh parsley, to the egg mixture or sprinkling paprika on top of the cooked egg will give it extra flavour.

Extra-thick Porridge

Porridge is a really healthy breakfast for all the family but it can be tricky for babies to manage. This extra-thick version can be picked up in handfuls. (Your baby will also enjoy squeezing and smearing it, so a long-sleeved bib, or bare arms is a good idea.)

Serves 1 baby

3 level tbsp porridge oats (not 'instant' oat cereal; use jumbo rolled oats for a chunkier texture)
100ml (3½fl oz) water or milk, or a mixture of the two (according to your taste)

Put the oats into a small saucepan and add the water/milk. Bring to the boil and simmer for 5–6 minutes, stirring continuously. Allow to 'sit' for a few minutes, then serve warm. (You can also make porridge in a bowl in the microwave. Use the High setting and cook for about 2 minutes, stirring and checking every 30–60 seconds.)

Option

• Fruit is ideal for adding to porridge. However, if it is cooked with the porridge it usually stays hot for longer, so check the temperature of the fruit as well as the porridge before offering it to your baby. Try adding some grated apple or pear (with or without a pinch of cinnamon) during the cooking; a few fresh blueberries, or any stewed or puréed fruit (apricot, prunes, plums, apple, pear, etc.) during the cooking or stirred in afterwards; a little blackstrap molasses drizzled on top after cooking (this will make the porridge messier – but it does have lots of healthy B vitamins!).

Note: *If you want thinner porridge, just use more milk (or a mixture of milk and water).*

'Stewed plums, cooked with a cinnamon stick, has been a real winner. It's really good to freeze in ice-cubes and add to porridge in the morning.'

Jane, mother of Mia, 7 months

Quick Porridge Fingers

These little fingers are a very easy way for a baby just starting out to manage oats – although adults will probably want to stick to 'real' porridge. This recipe takes just a couple of minutes in the microwave, so it's great if you're in a hurry.

'Nils used to love quick porridge fingers – they seemed so plain to me but he could get hold of them and get quite a lot in, which he seemed to need at breakfast once he got to eight months or so. And I loved them because there was no mess first thing in the morning!'

Kate, mother of Nils, 2½ years

Serves 1 adult and 1 baby

3 level tbsp porridge oats (not 'instant' oat cereal)
3 tbsp milk

In a bowl, soak the oats in the milk until you have a mushy mixture.

Press the mixture into a small, flat-bottomed dish or bowl using the back of a spoon. Cook in the microwave for 2 minutes on High.

Cut into fingers while still hot and serve when cool.

Options

• Try pressing some ready-to-eat raisins or sultanas into the top of the oat mixture before you cook it.
• If you don't have a microwave, you can also make porridge fingers in the oven. Simply cook for about 15 minutes at 190°C/375°F/Gas Mark 5.

Drop Scones (Scotch Pancakes)

Drop scones are pancakes made with a slightly thicker version of simple pancake batter (see page 63). They can be served for breakfast or, with added fillings, for lunch or tea. Like all pancakes, they work best when the pan gets really hot – so don't be surprised if the first one isn't quite as good as the rest.

Makes up to 20 drop scones

125g (4½oz) self-raising flour (or 125g/4½oz plain flour
 plus 1 tsp baking powder)
1 egg
150ml (5fl oz) milk
oil (or butter, preferably unsalted) for frying

Put the flour into a mixing bowl, make a well in the centre of the flour and break the egg into it. Pour in half the milk then beat or whisk the ingredients together, starting in the middle and gradually working in the flour. Slowly add the remaining milk and continue beating until any lumps have disappeared and the consistency is like double cream. Stir in any additional ingredients (see options, below).

Heat a flat griddle or large non-stick frying pan with a very thin coating of oil. When the pan is really hot, pour in small amounts of batter – about 2 tbsp each time – so it spreads to 8–10cm (3–4in). Cook for a few minutes, until the edges are cooked and the top is set almost to the middle, then flip over the drop scone and cook it for the same length of time on the other side. If you have a big pan you can cook several drop scones at once.

Serve warm or cold, plain, or with a savoury or sweet spread.

> **Storage:** *Drop scones can be frozen; freeze them in an airtight container, separated with sheets of greaseproof paper so they don't stick together. They keep for a couple of months and can be reheated in seconds under a grill or in the microwave.*

Option

• You can add a little of anything you fancy to the mixture before cooking (take care though – too much will change the consistency). Try a little grated cheese (Cheddar or similar); some chopped spinach; some finely chopped red pepper; a few whole, ready-to-eat raisins; a few blueberries, squashed or cut in half; a little grated apple; or a little mashed banana.

On Toast ...

You can put pretty much anything on a piece of toast at breakfast time, but if you always go for jam or marmalade here are some healthier alternatives to offer your baby. Fingers of toast are probably the easiest shape to start off with – older babies and toddlers may prefer small triangles. Try some of the following toppings:

- Hummus (see page 73)
- Cheese
- Banana, mashed or sliced
- Sardines, in oil rather than brine (see page 67)
- Fish pâté
- Tomatoes, mashed or sliced
- Bean spread (see page 75)
- Baked beans, low-sugar and low-salt
- Smooth nut butter or peanut butter (so long as you don't suspect any allergies)
- Or even those portions of puréed vegetables that you made and froze before you heard of baby-led weaning!

Toast alternatives:
- White, wholemeal or granary bread – whichever you don't normally have (see page 163)
- Rye bread
- Fruit bread (see page 164–5)
- Pitta bread
- Chapattis (see page 167)
- English muffins, split in half (see page 169)
- Drop scones (see page 60)
- Croissants, low-salt
- Crumpets, low-salt
- Oat cakes, low-salt
- Rice cakes, low-salt

Tip: *Toasting the bread on one side only (under the grill rather than in a toaster) and putting spread on the untoasted side will help it to stick better and make the slice softer.*

61

LIGHT LUNCHES

Light meals are ideal for you and your baby at lunchtime or even at teatime, and this section has lots of ideas for meals that won't take too long to prepare and won't leave you feeling too full.

Cheese and Lentil Wedges

These tasty wedges are great for picnics or as a snack.

Serves 2 adults and 1 baby, generously

225g (8oz) red lentils, rinsed thoroughly in cold water and drained
450ml (16 fl oz) water
oil or butter (preferably unsalted) for frying
1 large onion, finely chopped
100g (3½oz) grated cheese
1 tsp dried mixed herbs
1 egg, beaten
25g (1oz) fresh breadcrumbs
freshly ground black pepper, to taste

Put the lentils into a pan with the water. Bring to the boil, then cover and simmer for 10–15 minutes until the lentils are soft and all the liquid is absorbed. Check occasionally and skim off any froth. Meanwhile, heat the oil or butter in a frying pan, add the onion and fry until soft.

Preheat the oven to 190°C/375°F/Gas Mark 5 and lightly grease a 23cm (9in) cake tin. Drain the lentils and the onion and put them into a mixing bowl. Add the other ingredients and mix well. Press into the prepared tin using the back of a spoon.

Oven bake for about 30 minutes. Allow to cool slightly, then cut into wedges. Serve warm or cold.

Pancakes

Pancakes are the classic light lunch or weekend breakfast, and once you've made them a few times you'll find them very quick and easy. Thin pancakes can be rolled up and then cut into pinwheels to make them more grabbable for babies. For thicker pancakes, just reduce the amount of milk (or milk and water). Experiment with the consistency to get your perfect pancake.

Makes about 15 pancakes

125g (4½oz) plain flour

1 egg

300ml (11fl oz) milk (or half-water, half-milk for a thinner pancake)

oil or butter (preferably unsalted) for frying

Tip: *Pancake batter can be used for Yorkshire puddings (see page 105) and Toad-in-the Hole (see page 102); it will keep for a few days in the fridge. Cooked pancakes can be frozen (separated with sheets of greaseproof paper) for up to two months.*

To make the batter, put the flour into a mixing bowl, make a well in the centre and break the egg into it. Pour in half the milk (or milk and water), and beat or whisk the ingredients together, starting in the middle and gradually working in the flour. Gradually add the rest of the liquid and continue beating until any lumps have disappeared and the consistency is like single cream. If you have time, leave the batter to rest for an hour or two in the fridge before cooking.

Next, heat a flat griddle or large frying pan with a very thin coating of oil or butter. When the pan is really hot, pour in a ladleful of batter and tilt the pan so it spreads out evenly and thinly. Allow to cook for about 3 minutes until bubbles are bursting over the whole surface. Gently lift around the edge to check that the underside is golden. At this point you should be able to jiggle the pan so that the whole pancake is loose. Flip the pancake over (toss it if you can!) and continue cooking for about 30 seconds.

Serve warm, either with a topping (see below) or a sauce. The simplest sauce is a squeeze of lemon juice or some natural yoghurt or crème fraîche.

Options

- For a richer batter, add 1–2 tsp of oil or melted butter.
- Try spreading one of the following on your pancake, before folding or rolling it up: ham or spinach with grated cheese; cream cheese; mashed banana; grated apple with raisins and cinnamon; or a few squashed blueberries or raspberries.

Bubble and Squeak

This traditional dish is great for babies once they are able to pick up handfuls of food and push it into their mouth. It's also a great way to use up leftover vegetables.

Serves 2 adults and 1 baby

about 450g (1lb) potatoes, cooked and mashed – leftovers work best
about 225g (8oz) cooked cabbage, chopped
pinch of freshly ground black pepper (optional)
½ tsp dried mixed herbs, or fresh equivalent (optional)
oil or butter (preferably unsalted) for frying

Put the mashed potato, cabbage, pepper and herbs into a bowl and mix well.

Heat the oil or butter in a frying pan, add the potato mixture to cover the base of the pan and flatten it so it's about 1–2cm (½–¾in) deep. Cook until the mixture is browned on the bottom, then turn it over and cook the other side, so it's browned on both sides and the middle is heated through. If you have a small pan you will need to cook the mixture in batches, adding a little more oil to the pan and pre-heating it each time. Alternatively, you can make individual patties of bubble and squeak by cooking small amounts separately.

Serve warm on its own, or it goes very well with baked beans, or as a side dish with cold chicken or turkey.

Options

- Although eggs don't appear in traditional bubble and squeak recipes, adding a beaten egg to the mixture will help bind it together and make it easier for your baby to hold.
- Adding ½ onion or 2 spring onions, finely chopped, then softened by frying gently in a little oil, will give some extra flavour.
- You can swap the cabbage for any pre-cooked, chopped or mashed vegetable (or combination of vegetables), for example: Brussels sprouts, curly kale, carrots, swede, parsnips, celery, butternut squash or courgettes.

Chickpea Patties

Chickpeas are very nutritious, and these patties are easy for a baby to hold and soft to eat. Making them with a blender is quickest, although you can also use a potato masher and wooden spoon.

Serves 2 adults and 1 baby

400g (14oz) tin chickpeas (or approx 100g/3½oz dried chickpeas, pre-cooked – see page 51)
3 garlic cloves, finely chopped or crushed (unless you are using a blender)
1–2 tsp ground coriander
1–2 tsp ground cumin
1 medium onion, chopped
juice of ½ lemon (approx 2 tbsp)
1 tbsp plain flour
approx 2 tbsp chopped fresh parsley
freshly ground black pepper, to taste
oil for frying

Rinse the chickpeas and drain them thoroughly. Combine them with the garlic, ground spices, onion and lemon juice in a large bowl and blend (or mash) thoroughly. Add the flour, parsley and black pepper and mix well.

Squeeze handfuls of the mixture into about 12 small patties (flouring or wetting your hands first will help to stop it sticking). Put them in the fridge for about 20 minutes to firm up.

Heat the oil in a frying pan until it is very hot, then add the patties and fry for a few minutes on each side until crisp.

Chickpea patties are best served warm, inside warmed pitta pockets or with strips of pitta bread with Hummus (see page 73), tahini, Yoghurt and Cucumber Dip (see page 74) or Spicy Tomato Salsa (see page 154).

Option

• If you want a spicier patty, you can add a pinch of chilli powder or some finely chopped chilli pepper to the mixture.

Easy Dahl

Dahl is a lovely, mild introduction to spicy food and has plenty of healthy nutrients. It makes a good dip but it can also be eaten with a spoon or picked up in handfuls. If your baby is just starting out, offer her some ready-loaded dippers.

Serves 2 adults and 1 baby

oil, ghee or butter (preferably unsalted) for frying
1–2 medium onions, chopped
2 garlic cloves, finely chopped or crushed
½ tsp turmeric
½ tsp ground cumin
½ tsp mild chilli powder or chilli flakes, to taste
1–2cm (½–¾in) piece of fresh ginger, peeled and finely
    chopped or grated (optional)
225g (8oz) yellow or red lentils, rinsed thoroughly in
    cold water and drained
1 cinnamon stick or ½ tsp ground cinnamon (optional)
approx 750ml (26fl oz) water
juice of ½ lemon (approx 2 tbsp) (optional)
1 tbsp fresh coriander leaves, chopped

Heat the oil or butter in a pan, add the onion and fry until soft. Add the garlic and fry for another minute or two, then stir in the powdered spices and the ginger (if using). Add the lentils and cinnamon (if using), with enough water to cover them. Bring to the boil, stirring occasionally, then turn down the heat, cover and simmer for 25–30 minutes, continuing to stir occasionally until the lentils are soft but not mushy.

Remove the cinnamon stick (if using), add the lemon juice and stir well. Sprinkle with the chopped coriander and serve warm with other curries, Yoghurt and Cucumber Dip (see page 74) and rice, naan bread or chapattis (see page 167). Alternatively, use as a dip, with strips of pitta or chapatti, or sticks of vegetables.

Option

• You can also make dahl with yellow split peas, although these take longer to cook.

Tuna Croquettes

These little croquettes are delicious and really easy for babies to handle; they can also be made with salmon.

Serves 2 adults and 1 baby, generously

2 large potatoes
185g (6½oz) tin tuna (in oil or spring water, not brine)
juice of 1 lime (approx 1 tbsp), or to taste
25g (1oz) butter (preferably unsalted)
25–50g (1–2oz) breadcrumbs (preferably stale or toasted)

> **Storage:** *Cooked tuna croquettes keep for a couple of days in the fridge or they can be frozen. They can be reheated in a micro-wave or in the oven.*

Peel the potatoes and cut into small pieces and put them on to steam or boil.

Preheat the oven to 200°C/400°F/Gas Mark 6 and lightly grease a large baking sheet. Drain the tuna and break it up.

When the potatoes are cooked, drain and mash them and add the tuna. Add the lime juice and mix well. Stir in the butter.

Shape the mixture into small sausages (flouring or wetting your hands will help to stop it sticking), then roll each one in the breadcrumbs and put on to the baking sheet. Bake in the oven for about 20 minutes, until browned and cooked through.

Serve warm, with vegetables, such as green beans and sweetcorn.

Sardines on Toast

This is a simple, healthy lunch or teatime meal, made with plain tinned sardines in oil (rather than the ones that come in a tomato sauce, which are usually quite salty).

Serves 2 adults and 1 baby

125g (4½oz) tin sardines (in olive oil)
6–8 ripe cherry tomatoes, roughly chopped
6–8 fresh basil leaves, chopped (to taste)
bread for toasting (preferably rye or wholemeal)
juice of ½ lemon (approx 2 tbsp) (optional)

Preheat the grill to Medium. Drain the sardines and mash them (including the soft bones) with a fork. Add the tomatoes and mix well. Add the basil and stir well.

Put the bread under the grill and toast it on one side only. Spread the sardine mixture on the untoasted side, then put it back under the grill until warmed through.

Add a squeeze of lemon juice, if you like. Cut into fingers or triangles while still hot and serve warm, with salad or Spicy Tomato Salsa (see page 154).

Baked Potatoes

Baked potatoes are an excellent standby for lunch. They are best cooked slowly, in the oven, but they can also be cooked in about 10 minutes in a microwave.

> **1 large baking potato per person (the person with the biggest one**
> **gets to share with the baby)**
> **1 small knob of butter (preferably unsalted) per potato (optional)**
> **topping of your choice (see below)**

Preheat the oven to 200°C/400°F/Gas Mark 6. Choose potatoes of roughly similar sizes, scrub them thoroughly, dry them, and prick them all over with a fork. Put them in the oven (they don't need a tray) and bake for about 1 hour, depending on their size (when done, they should feel soft when squeezed).

Baked potatoes are best served warm, with a knob of butter or a topping, and a side salad. Cut the potato into wedges for your baby, or split it wide open and let him help himself to soft handfuls of potato and topping. Alternatively, scoop out the inside of the potato, mix with the topping, then pile it all back into the skin.

Options

- Brushing the potatoes with oil before putting them in the oven makes the skins shiny and less dry.
- Sweet potatoes can also be baked (for slightly less time), but they tend to drip, so put them on a tray.
- Ideas for toppings: grated or cream cheese; baked beans; tuna with sweetcorn; mackerel with tomatoes; chilli con carne; Bolognese sauce; cooked beetroot with feta cheese.

Tip: *Pushing a metal skewer through each potato (and leaving it in place) before putting them in the oven will reduce the cooking time.*

Pesto Pitta Pockets

This simple recipe is just right for babies who can deal with chewier textures.

pitta bread pockets
1 tsp pesto sauce (low-salt, or home-made –
see page 184) per pocket
10–15g (¼–½oz) grated cheese per pocket

Tip: *Toasting the pitta pockets lightly in a toaster first can make them easier to open.*

Preheat the grill to Medium. Open up the pitta pockets and spread the pesto on the inside surfaces. Scatter the cheese on top of the pesto. Close the pockets and grill or microwave them for a few minutes, until the cheese has melted.

Cut into fingers (for your baby) while still hot and serve warm.

Pizza Toast

This is a cross between cheese on toast and a pizza; cut into fingers it's very easy for even beginner BLW babies to eat. The topping is great for wraps, too.

1 slice of bread (or more) per person
1 tsp tomato purée (salt-free) per toast
15–25g (½–1oz) cheese, grated per toast
sprinkling of dried oregano (or mixed herbs) per toast

Preheat the grill to High. Toast (or grill) the bread on one side only. With the untoasted side up, spread the tomato purée on the bread and scatter the cheese and oregano evenly on top. Cook under the grill until the cheese has melted.

Cut into fingers or triangles (for your baby) while still hot and serve warm.

Options

• Add your favourite toppings – chopped ham, mushrooms, tuna, fresh tomatoes, etc. – just as you would with a traditional pizza.
• You can use a split English muffin instead of toast. For a crispy base, bake the muffin pizzas in the oven at 160°C/325°F/Gas Mark 3 for 10–15 minutes, rather than grilling.

Arancini

Arancini are a delicious, easy finger food made from freshly made or leftover risotto (see page 142). They are traditionally filled with ham or mozzarella cheese. True arancini are little balls, but you can make unfilled ones stick shaped if you prefer. To save leftover risotto so you can make arancini the next day, spread it in a shallow dish immediately after cooking so it cools as quickly as possible. When it's completely cool, transfer the risotto to an airtight container and put it in the fridge.

If you are making risotto just so you can make arancini, it's probably best to keep the recipe fairly simple – maybe just onion, garlic and Parmesan cheese, together with the rice. Allow the cooked risotto to cool before you start to handle it.

Arancini sticks (and balls cut in half) make great dippers.

Serves 2 adults and 1 baby

a little flour for coating

1 egg, beaten

50g (2oz) breadcrumbs, preferably stale or baked

2 mugfuls cooked risotto, with any large chunks of other
  ingredients (such as chicken or carrots) removed

some small pieces of mozzarella or ham (optional)

2 tbsp oil for frying

Put the flour, egg and breadcrumbs into three separate bowls. With wet hands, take about 1 tbsp of risotto in the palm of your hand. Squash and mould it into a ball about the size of a golf ball, an oval or a short stick shape.

If you are filling the arancini, mould a ball and then make a hole in it with your finger. Gently push in a small piece of mozzarella and/or a small piece of ham, then press around the filling to cover it completely with the rice.

Dip each shape in flour, then into the beaten egg, and then into the breadcrumbs, so that it is coated thoroughly.

Heat the oil in a large frying pan, and when hot, add the arancini and cook for 5–10 minutes, turning them occasionally, until they're golden and crisp.

Serve warm. If you have filled the arancini with mozzarella, cut the balls in half before offering them to your baby and check that the cheese is not too hot.

Onigiri (Japanese Rice Balls)

Onigiri are very popular in Japan and are often put into lunchboxes or taken on picnics. They can be made plain or with a filling, such as grilled salmon, and wrapped in a strip of nori (edible seaweed) to add a different flavour and texture. Traditionally round or triangular, they can be made into any shape or size to suit your baby.

Sushi rice is the best rice for making onigiri but you can use sticky rice or risotto rice instead. You can buy nori in any Japanese or Chinese grocery shop, and in many major supermarkets.

Serves 2 adults and 1 baby

250g (9oz) (about ¾ of a mugful) Japanese sushi rice
filling of your choice, in small pieces (e.g. salmon, avocado,
   tinned tuna)
1–2 sheets of nori, cut into strips (optional)

Cook the rice according to the instructions on the packet and allow to cool slightly.

With wet hands, take 1–2 tbsp of warm rice and press into your cupped hand (or a small bowl), making a dent in the middle. Put in your chosen filling and mould the rice around it, pressing firmly and ensuring that the filling is completely covered.

Make the onigiri into a ball, sausage shape or triangle, to suit your baby, applying enough force, and adding a little warm water if needed, to stick the grains together firmly (or it will crumble). If you want, you can then wrap the onigiri with a strip of nori.

Serve warm or cold, on their own or with a dip.

Option

• Adults may like their onigiri filled with ume (pickled plum), which is very salty and so not suitable for babies and young children.

DIPS & SPREADS

O ffering your baby soft food as a dip, along with a 'dipper' to eat it with, is a great way to help him begin to master the skills he'll need for cutlery. Dippers can be foods that a baby can eat (even without teeth), such as breadsticks, or they can be harder foods, which he won't eat but will suck or lick. A stick of celery is ideal because it is similar to a spoon – it can hold a lot of dip and will encourage your baby to use his tongue to scoop it out. Babies can use a spoon to dip with too – or their fingers. They usually start discovering how dippers work any time from around eight months, although some get the hang of it sooner. Be prepared – dips can be very messy when your baby is learning how to eat them.

'Blake's favourite lunch was hummus, carrot sticks and pitta, for ages. We started with strips of pitta spread with hummus, and then once he discovered how to dunk the pitta or carrot in the hummus he was well away. He still loves it.'

Leah, mother of Blake, 19 months

Foods that make good dippers:

- Breadsticks
- Strips or wedges of pitta
- Toast fingers
- Sticks of raw vegetable, such as red pepper, cucumber, celery, courgette and carrot
- Sticks or wedges of fruit, such as apple, nectarine and mango

Hummus

Hummus is a really nutritious dip, and most babies love it. It can be eaten with warm pitta bread – cut into strips or wedges, or halved – or with raw vegetable sticks or breadsticks as dippers. It's lovely with salad and it makes a tasty filling for baked potatoes. It's also good in sandwiches, or on toast or oatcakes. Try it on freshly baked ciabatta bread rolls, with grated carrot and cheese, too.

> **400g (14oz) tin chickpeas (or approx 100g/3½oz dried chickpeas, pre-cooked – see page 51)**
> **1–2 garlic cloves, finely chopped or crushed**
> **juice of 1 lemon (approx 4 tbsp)**
> **approx 2 tbsp tahini (sesame seed paste)**
> **2–3 tbsp olive oil**
> **pinch of paprika**

Rinse and drain the chickpeas and mash them with a potato masher (or use a blender or food processor). Add a little of the garlic, lemon juice, tahini and olive oil and mix thoroughly.

Taste the hummus to see if it needs more garlic, lemon juice or tahini; add more oil if you want a smoother texture.

Transfer the hummus to a serving dish and sprinkle with paprika. Chill in the fridge before serving.

Options

- Try adding some ground black pepper or a pinch of cumin along with the garlic and lemon juice.
- Chopped fresh herbs, such as parsley or coriander, can also be added, for a tasty variation.
- Add 1 tbsp of natural yoghurt or crème fraîche for a creamier dip.

> **Storage:** *Hummus keeps well in the fridge (covered) for 2–3 days.*

Guacamole

Guacamole can be served as a dip or as a spread on toast, rice cakes or oat cakes but it quickly goes brown, so it needs to be eaten within an hour or two.

> **2 ripe medium tomatoes, blanched, skinned and cooled**
> **1 ripe avocado, cut in half, with the stone removed**
> **juice of 1 lemon (approx 4 tbsp)**
> **½ garlic clove, finely chopped or crushed**
> **2 tsp soured cream or crème fraîche (optional)**
> **1 tsp chopped fresh coriander (optional)**

Chop the tomatoes finely. Scoop the avocado flesh out of the skin, put it into a bowl and mash with a fork. Mix in the lemon juice, garlic, tomatoes and soured cream or crème fraîche (if using).

Sprinkle with the chopped coriander (if using) and serve immediately.

Yoghurt and Cucumber Dip

This is the perfect dip to serve with a spicy curry, raw vegetable sticks or chickpea patties (see page 65).

> **½ medium cucumber, peeled and deseeded**
> **200g (7oz) natural yoghurt (preferably live)**
> **1 small red onion, finely chopped**
> **1 tbsp fresh lemon juice (or 1 tsp fresh lime juice)**
> **1–2 tbsp fresh coriander, coarsely chopped**
> **freshly ground black pepper**

Grate the cucumber into a bowl and add the yoghurt, onion, lemon (or lime) juice and coriander. Stir well, add black pepper to taste and chill before serving.

Tip: *Cucumber is easier to grate when it's in one piece, so if you prefer you can leave the seeds in, then drain it once grated. You can also leave the skin on to provide a bit of extra colour and texture.*

Options

- For serving with a curry, add ¼ tsp of ground cumin, or a pinch of ground nutmeg, cinnamon or cardamom.
- For serving with chickpea patties or as a dip, try adding 2 cloves of garlic (finely chopped or crushed) and replacing the coriander with chopped fresh mint or dill.

Bean Spread

This spread is great as a dip, in sandwiches, or spread on toast or rice cakes.

> ½ x 400g (14oz) tin red kidney beans, butter beans or haricot
>   beans (or 50g/2oz dried beans, pre-cooked – see page 51)
> 1 small onion, roughly chopped
> 1 medium carrot, cooked
> 1–2 tsp tomato purée
> ½ tsp dried mixed herbs
> 2 tsp cider vinegar
> 1–2 tsp oil

Put all the ingredients into a blender or food processor and blend to a smooth paste (or mash thoroughly with a potato masher). Chill before serving.

Salmon Spread

This spread is very nutritious and can be served on toast, oat cakes or rice cakes, or with a little salad.

> 185g (6½oz) tin salmon (in oil or spring water, not brine),
>   drained thoroughly, with skin and any bones removed
> 200g (7oz) ricotta cheese
> juice of ½ lemon (approx 2 tbsp)
> 2 tbsp natural yoghurt (preferably live)
> freshly ground black pepper

Put all the ingredients into a bowl and stir thoroughly until smooth and well combined (or use an electric blender or food processor).

Option
• You can make a similar spread using tinned mackerel, sardines or tuna.

Baba Ganoush (Aubergine Dip)

Baba ganoush is best served as a dip but it also makes a delicious spread (on toast or rice cakes) or a filling for baked potato.

> 1 medium aubergine (whole)
> juice of 1 lemon (approx 4 tbsp)
> 1 garlic clove, peeled
> 1 tbsp tahini (sesame seed paste)
> pinch of chilli powder (optional)
> pinch of ground cumin
> pinch of freshly ground black pepper
> a little olive oil
> 2 tsp fresh parsley, coarsely chopped

Preheat the oven to 200°C/400°F/Gas Mark 6 and lightly grease a baking sheet. Pierce the skin of the aubergine in several places with a fork and put it on the baking sheet. Bake for about 30–40 minutes, until the skin has blistered, turning the aubergine over after about 15 minutes to ensure even cooking. Remove from the oven and allow to cool, then peel and put in a colander. Allow to drain thoroughly for 10–15 minutes.

Cut the drained aubergine into a few large pieces and put it into a food processor with all the other ingredients, except the olive oil and parsley. Blend thoroughly or use a bowl and a hand-held blender if you prefer.

Chill, then drizzle with olive oil and sprinkle with the parsley before serving.

Options
• Add 1 tbsp of natural yoghurt for a creamier dip.

SOUPS

Don't be afraid to offer your baby soup, even though it won't be the easiest thing for her to eat at first. Many naturally thick soups, such as butternut squash soup, can be made thicker still, or she may be able to eat it with a dipper (see page 18) or a spoon pre-loaded by you. Some soups can be left chunky and unblended, so your baby can fish out pieces of food. Or you can add cooked rice, pasta or small pieces of bread to the soup, to make it easier for her to pick it up in soft handfuls. However, you may need to hold on to your baby's bowl, if she isn't used to using one, or buy one that sticks to the table, so the whole lot doesn't get tipped over. Don't forget to check that the soup has cooled down before putting it in front of her.

A large pan of soup takes about the same time to make as a small one, so you might want to make double quantities of these recipes and freeze some for later.

'Ashton used to eat lots of soup just by dipping pieces of bread into it – and by 15 months he'd eat soup by using a spoon half the time and then dunking bread the rest. He really enjoys his soup.'

Jackie, mother of Ashton, 2 years

Thick Butternut Squash Soup

Butternut squash is deliciously sweet and has a soft texture, making it ideal for soups – but you can use any other firm squash or pumpkin for this recipe.

Serves 2 adults and 1 baby

oil or butter (preferably unsalted) for frying
1 medium onion, finely chopped
1 medium butternut squash, peeled, deseeded and cubed
1 garlic clove, finely chopped or crushed
1 tsp garam masala
1 tsp ground cumin (optional)
500–600ml (18–21fl oz) chicken or vegetable stock (low-salt or
    home-made, see pages 182–3)
freshly ground black pepper, to taste

Heat the oil or butter in a large pan and fry the onion until just soft. Add the squash, garlic, garam masala and cumin (if using), and fry gently for a few minutes, stirring so that nothing sticks to the bottom of the pan or burns. Add the stock, bring to the boil, then cover and simmer for 30 minutes.

Check that the squash is soft, then blend to a smooth soup in a blender or food processor and add black pepper to taste. If it isn't thick enough for your baby to manage, cook uncovered for a further 5–10 minutes.

Serve warm with chunks of fresh bread or toast.

Options

- Fresh grated ginger or some chilli flakes can be added with the garlic, to make a spicier soup.
- You can add chunks of carrots or sweet potatoes with the butternut squash to make a more richly flavoured soup.

Thick Lentil Soup

This rich soup gets much of its flavour from the chorizo, which is fairly salty, so it's okay to eat occasionally but not every day. It's thick enough for a baby to get quite a lot with a dipper. Chopping the chorizo into thin sticks makes it curly when cooked, which is great fun for babies.

Serves 2 adults and 1 baby

up to 50g (2oz) chorizo sausage (preferably unsliced)
oil or butter (preferably unsalted) for frying
½ medium onion, sliced
1 garlic clove, finely chopped or crushed
125g (4½oz) red lentils, rinsed thoroughly in cold water and
    drained
1 bay leaf
500–600ml (18–21fl oz) water, or chicken or vegetable stock
    (low-salt or home-made, see pages 182–3)

If your chorizo is unsliced, chop it into thin sticks, approx 5cm (2in) long.

Heat the oil or butter in a large pan and fry the onion until just soft. Add the garlic and chorizo and fry for a few more minutes. Add the lentils and cook for 1–2 minutes. Add the bay leaf and top up with enough water or stock to treble the volume of the ingredients in the pan. Bring to the boil, then cover and simmer for 45 minutes, until the lentils are soft. If it is not thick enough, take the lid off and simmer for a further 5 minutes.

Serve warm with chunks of fresh bread or toast.

Chicken Soup

This is a lovely soup to make with the remains of a roast chicken. You can leave the solid ingredients as chunks for your baby to pick up, or you can blend everything to make a smooth soup. You can then either show your baby how to dip bread into it or offer her pieces of soaked bread.

Serves 2 adults and 1 baby

oil or butter (preferably unsalted) for frying

1 small onion, chopped

1–2 garlic cloves, finely chopped or crushed

up to 100g (3½oz) cooked chicken

1 large carrot, cut to suit your baby

1 small parsnip, cut to suit your baby

1 small celery stick, cut to suit your baby

1 small handful of frozen peas

1–2 tbsp puy or red lentils, rinsed thoroughly in cold water and
    drained

1 sprig of fresh thyme (or a pinch of dried)

freshly ground black pepper

1 litre (1¾pt) chicken or vegetable stock (low-salt or home-made –
    see pages 182–3)

Heat the oil or butter in a large pan, add the onion and fry until soft. Add the garlic and fry for another minute or two. Add the cooked chicken, prepared vegetables, peas, lentils, thyme and black pepper. Pour in the stock and bring to the boil. Reduce the heat, cover, and simmer for 20 minutes.

Blend the soup with an electric blender or leave it as it is, depending on what is easier for your baby. Serve warm, with chunks of fresh bread.

SALADS

Most salads are full of vitamins and minerals. They are particularly good for babies who are progressing with baby-led weaning because they contain lots of different shapes and textures to pick up, examine, and then test out with gums and teeth.

'Daniela hasn't really worked out what to do with salads yet. She's very interested but she just plays with bits – she'll chew a leaf, but the whole thing will come back out again.'

Paola, mother of Alessandra, 3 years, and Daniela, 8 months

Raw salads

Raw salad doesn't have to mean just lettuce, tomato and cucumber; many vegetables, such as carrot, beetroot and courgette, can be eaten raw (babies can often manage them grated), and fruit such as strawberries and oranges (in segments or chunks) are delicious with a balsamic dressing.

Don't expect your baby to eat lots of raw salad leaves at first, because she won't be able to chew them very effectively – but she will almost certainly want to have a go. She will, however, probably enjoy sticks of cucumber or red pepper.

Raw salad ingredients need to be thoroughly washed. To dry salad leaves (such as lettuce, rocket and watercress), shake them over the sink or inside a clean tea towel, or use a salad spinner.

Cooked salads

Simple, delicious salads can be made using many different vegetables, eaten warm or at room temperature. When cooked, simply drain them and add a dressing (see page 90). Roasted summer vegetables (see pages 150–1), home-cooked or tinned red kidney beans or butter beans, lightly steamed green beans or mangetout, and steamed or boiled potatoes (especially new potatoes) or beetroot are all great in salads.

You can also make a salad using cold cooked rice, couscous or bulgur wheat, together with some vegetables or fruit.

Croutons

Croutons go well with many salads and they add yet another texture for your baby to try. They are very easy to make: all you need is one slice of bread per person and about 1 tbsp of olive oil (preferably extra virgin). Preheat the oven to 200°C/400°F/Gas Mark 6. Cut the bread into cubes (with some finger shapes or small triangles for your baby) and put them on a baking sheet. Brush the shapes all over with olive oil, then bake them in the oven for about 5 minutes, until golden brown.

Potato Salad

This is a great salad for babies who are just getting started – you can easily cut the potatoes and cucumber into shapes that your baby will be able to pick up (see page 25), and the crème fraîche makes the mixture sticky, rather than slippery. Potato salad goes particularly well with fish such as salmon and mackerel.

Serves 2 adults and 1 baby

125ml (4fl oz) crème fraîche
½–1 garlic clove, finely chopped or crushed
1 tbsp chopped fresh chives
freshly ground black pepper, to taste
500g (1lb 2oz) new potatoes, cooked, cooled and cut to suit your baby
¼ medium cucumber, peeled and cut to suit your baby

Combine the crème fraîche, garlic, chives and black pepper. Add the cooked potatoes and cucumber and stir well. As this salad contains crème fraîche and garlic, it can be served as it is, without any additional dressing.

Options

- Adults may prefer to chop their cucumber into small chunks, rather than sticks. If you want to do this, simply add the cucumber in sticks to your baby's portion, and the chopped cucumber to the rest.
- You can swap the chives for a little chopped dill or parsley.

Roast Carrot, Bean and Feta Salad

This salad offers lots of different shapes for your baby to explore. If she is just starting to pick up things with her thumb and forefinger (the pincer grip) butter beans are ideal to practise with; if she's a BLW beginner she'll enjoy the baby carrots and green beans.

Serves 2 adults and 1 baby

2 tbsp olive oil
500g (1lb 2oz) small whole baby carrots (cut any larger ones in
    half lengthways)
1 sprig of fresh lemon thyme (optional)
freshly ground black pepper, to taste
100g (3½oz) green beans, trimmed and cut in half
½ x 400g (14oz) tin butter or cannellini beans, rinsed and drained
    (or approx 50g/2oz dried, pre-cooked beans, see page 51)
½ small red onion, finely sliced
100g (3½oz) feta cheese, crumbled
1 small bunch of fresh mint, chopped

Preheat the oven to 220°C/425°F/Gas Mark 7. Put half the oil into a large roasting tin and heat, either in the oven or on the hob. Put the carrots into the roasting tin with the lemon thyme (if using). Toss the carrots to coat them with the oil, sprinkle them with black pepper then roast in the oven for 20–30 minutes until the carrots are tender, turning them halfway through cooking.

Meanwhile, steam the green beans for about 5 minutes until tender. Drain, rinse immediately with cold water, then drain thoroughly.

Mix together the green beans, butter or cannellini beans, remaining oil, onion and feta, and add black pepper to taste. Mix in the hot carrots, then sprinkle with the mint just before serving.

Serve as it is, or with a dressing of your choice (see page 90).

Option

• You can use Lancashire cheese instead of feta; it has a similar texture but is less salty.

Chicken Caesar Salad

This Caesar salad is made with strips of chicken, which are ideal for babies just starting out. The anchovies that are traditionally included in a Caesar dressing are too salty for babies, but adults may like to add them to their portion. The basic French dressing (see page 90) is an integral part of this recipe, so we've repeated it here.

Serves 2 adults and 1 baby

oil or butter (preferably unsalted) for frying

2–3 chicken breasts, cut into strips

2 heads (or hearts) crispy lettuce (such as romaine or baby cos),
  washed and drained

2 handfuls of croutons (see page 82)

approx 25g (1oz) Parmesan cheese, grated or thinly sliced

For the dressing:

1 garlic clove, finely chopped or crushed

2 tbsp olive oil (preferably extra virgin)

2 tsp lemon juice or white wine vinegar

freshly ground black pepper, to taste

Heat the oil or butter in a pan and fry the chicken strips for 5–10 minutes, turning occasionally, until cooked through (check by cutting one in half), then drain on kitchen paper and set aside.

Thoroughly mix together all the dressing ingredients and put into a large bowl. Toss the lettuce leaves in the dressing. Add the chicken strips and croutons and mix lightly.

You can serve this salad with the chicken warm or cold, or you can use cold, ready-cooked chicken breast from your roast dinner. No additional dressing is needed. Divide among individual plates and top with Parmesan cheese.

Orange and Watercress Salad

This recipe uses a dressing made with cider vinegar, which goes especially well with oranges. Chicory has a very distinctive, bitter flavour which your baby might enjoy trying. This salad is ideal for babies with a little dexterity, but even a baby who's just beginning to feed herself will enjoy picking up the orange segments and will get a taste of the orange combined with the dressing.

Serves 2 adults and 1 baby

1 orange
1 baby chicory head
50g (2oz) watercress
1 tbsp chopped fresh coriander (optional)

For the dressing:
2 tbsp olive oil (preferably extra virgin)
2 tsp cider vinegar
freshly ground black pepper, to taste

Peel the orange carefully, removing all the pith. Either cut the flesh into chunks or separate it into segments (if you can, remove the thin skin from each segment). Try to catch any orange juice that escapes, to add to the dressing.

Separate the chicory leaves and break the watercress into short pieces.

Thoroughly mix together the dressing ingredients, plus any collected orange juice, and put into a large bowl. Add the orange, chicory and watercress and toss them in the dressing. Sprinkle with the chopped coriander and serve.

This salad goes well with cold chicken or pork. It needs no additional dressing.

Option

• If you find chicory too bitter, you can use Chinese leaves instead.

Tuscan Salad

The grilled peppers in this recipe are deliciously sweet and soft. They are also quite slippery, providing your baby with lots of practice at dealing with a tricky texture to hold on to. The beans are good for when she's learning to pick things up with her thumb and finger (the pincer grip).

Serves 2 adults and 1 baby

1 red pepper, deseeded and cut into 6–8 long strips
1 yellow pepper, deseeded and cut into 6–8 long strips
approx 150g (5½oz) bread, preferably ciabatta
French dressing with garlic (see page 90) (optional)
3 ripe fresh plum tomatoes, cut into quarters
400g (14oz) tin cannellini beans, rinsed and
drained (or approx 100g /3½oz dried beans,
pre-cooked – see page 51)
3–4 black olives (in oil, not brine), stones
removed and thinly sliced
handful of fresh basil leaves, torn

Preheat the grill to High. Grill the peppers, skin-side up, for about 5 minutes, so that all the skin is thoroughly charred, then allow to cool. When cool, remove the skins and cut the flesh into strips.

Cut the bread into rough fingers for your baby and smaller cubes for the adults and grill, turning once, until lightly toasted (or use a toaster and cut after toasting).

Put the dressing (if using) into a salad bowl; add the grilled peppers, tomatoes, beans, olives and basil, and toss well. Top with the toasted bread.

Tuscan salad goes well with goat's cheese or Brie.

Options

- If your baby can manage them, a couple of tbsp of toasted pine nuts make a tasty addition and provide a different texture. It's probably best to avoid Chinese and Korean pine nuts as these can occasionally leave a bitter aftertaste.
- Capers are delicious with this salad but they tend to be salty, so they are not really suitable for babies – but you may like to add them to your own plate.

Goat's Cheese Salad

Goat's cheese has a very distinctive flavour that may be interesting for your baby to try – and there's plenty here for babies who are just starting out, including soft, roasted peppers without their skins.

Serves 2 adults and 1 baby

1 red pepper, deseeded and cut into 6–8 long strips
200g (7oz) soft goat's cheese (sometimes labelled chèvre blanc – usually about 7cm/3in diameter)
4 slices bread
a little olive oil
freshly ground black pepper
approx 2 tbsp salad dressing (French dressing with added garlic works well – see page 90)
2–3 handfuls mixed green salad leaves, washed and drained (e.g. lettuce, rocket, watercress, spinach)

Preheat the grill to High. Grill the pepper, skin-side up, for about 5 minutes so that all the skin is thoroughly charred, then allow to cool.

Cut the cheese into four thin slices and use a pastry cutter to cut the bread into circles roughly the same diameter as the cheese. Toast the bread on both sides, then put a piece of cheese on top of each slice.

Drizzle a little olive oil and some black pepper (to taste) onto the cheese and grill for about 2 minutes.

Meanwhile, skin the peppers and cut them into strips. Put the dressing into a salad bowl, add the salad leaves and strips of pepper and toss them in the dressing.

Put the salad on a wide flat plate and arrange the slices of goat's cheese on toast on the top. Serve while the goat's cheese is still warm. The toast can be cut into wedge or finger shapes for your baby.

Colourful Stir-fry Salad

This delicious salad has lots of different colours, textures and tastes for your baby to explore, and is particularly good for babies whose teeth are appearing and who are beginning to enjoy crunchy textures.

Serves 2 adults and 1 baby

2 handfuls mixed salad leaves, washed and drained (e.g. lettuce,
    rocket, watercress, spinach or mizuna, Japanese salad leaves)
½ orange pepper, deseeded and cut into thin sticks
½ yellow pepper, deseeded and cut into thin sticks
6 cherry tomatoes, cut in half
½ medium avocado, stone removed
a little sesame oil for frying
½ tbsp mustard seeds (optional)
6 baby sweetcorn, cut in half lengthways
1 medium beetroot (raw), peeled and cut into thin sticks
1 medium carrot, cut into thin sticks

Put the salad leaves into a large salad bowl and add the peppers and tomatoes.

Cut the avocado flesh into strips, leaving some of the skin on to make it easier for your baby to grip. Add to the bowl with the peppers and tomatoes.

Heat a large pan (preferably a wok) until very hot and add the oil and mustard seeds (if using). When the seeds start to pop, add the baby corn, beetroot and carrot, and stir-fry for a few minutes. Keep the pan very hot and keep stirring the vegetables. Cook until just tender (or a little softer if your baby has no teeth yet), then add to the salad bowl.

This salad is especially good served with a helping of croutons and a little extra sesame oil.

Option

• 1 tbsp of toasted sesame seeds added
  to the salad gives a distinctive
  flavour.

Cheesy Tuna and Sweetcorn Pasta Salad

This is a great BLW dish as the tuna and cheese stick to the pasta, so it's easy to eat. And once your baby is developing her pincer grip she will enjoy practising it on the pieces of sweetcorn.

Serves 2 adults and 1 baby

225g (8oz) pasta (fusilli works best)

185g (6½oz) tin tuna (in oil or spring water, not brine)

½ x 270g (9½oz) tin sweetcorn

50–75g (2–2½oz) cream cheese, such as Philadelphia or mascarpone

Cook the pasta in a pan of boiling water according to the instructions on the packet, then drain, rinse with cold water, drain again, and allow to cool.

Meanwhile, break the tuna into flakes, add the sweetcorn and cream cheese and mix well. Add the cooled pasta and stir to combine. Serve immediately or put in the fridge until later.

This dish should be served cold and is good with extra cucumber sticks, sliced peppers (red, orange, yellow or green) and tomato wedges (or halved cherry tomatoes).

Salad Dressings

Most salads can be served with just a little good-quality extra virgin olive oil and a sprinkling of black pepper, but many can be transformed by a good dressing. The basic dressings below will go with most salads. An easy way to mix the ingredients is to put everything into a small jar, put the lid on and shake vigorously. (The oil will separate out between uses – just shake to remix.)

Salad dressings will usually keep for a week or two in the fridge, so it's a good idea to make up enough for several salads in one go.

Note: Mayonnaise is not recommended for babies because most brands contain raw egg; however, egg-free mayonnaise is available in some larger supermarkets or health-food shops.

Lemon and oil dressing

Combine 2 tbsp olive oil (preferably extra virgin) with the juice of 1 lemon (approx 4 tbsp). If you like, you can add 1–2 tsp chopped fresh mint or a little grated fresh ginger.

French dressing

Combine 2 tbsp olive oil (preferably extra virgin) with 2 tsp lemon juice or white (or red) wine vinegar and some freshly ground black pepper to taste. You can also add 1 tsp Dijon or wholegrain mustard, 1–2 crushed garlic cloves or a couple of teaspoons of chopped fresh herbs, such as chives, mint or parsley and thyme.

Balsamic dressing

Combine 2 tbsp balsamic vinegar with 3–4 tbsp olive oil (preferably extra virgin) and, if you like, 1 tbsp finely chopped fresh basil or coriander.

Soured cream dressing

Combine 140ml (5fl oz) carton soured cream or natural yoghurt with 2 tbsp white wine vinegar, ¼ finely chopped onion and a pinch of freshly ground black pepper. (This dressing goes especially well with potato or beetroot salads.)

MAINS: MEAT

Meat is an easy first food for your baby – especially if it's tender. Stews and slow-cooked dishes are ideal, and home-made sausages, burgers and patties are easy for babies to pick up and chew.

Home-made Beef Burgers

These tasty burgers are much healthier than the fast-food version, and can be cut into wedges when cooked to make them easy for your baby to handle. Serve with hamburger buns or English muffins, sliced tomato, raw onion and Spicy Tomato Salsa (see page 154). They are also good with potato wedges or couscous, and salad.

Serves 2 adults and 1 baby

500g (1lb 2oz) lean minced beef
1 small onion, finely chopped
1 egg, beaten
1 tsp Dijon mustard (optional)
1 tbsp chopped fresh parsley or coriander (optional)
oil for frying (if needed)

Put all the ingredients into a bowl and mix thoroughly. Shape the mixture into balls about the size of tennis balls (flouring or wetting your hands will help to stop it sticking), then flatten them into burgers, making sure they are all roughly the same thickness. If you have time, cover the burgers and put them in the fridge to firm up for an hour or so (or until you're ready to cook them).

Heat a griddle or frying pan, with oil if needed, and fry the burgers for 5–8 minutes on each side, pressing them down if griddling, until cooked through (check by cutting one in half – there should be no pink meat). Serve warm.

Beef and Broccoli Stir-fry

'Lucien has still only got two teeth, but he'll suck on strips or chunks of meat, chew it and spit bits out. For a couple of weeks he hardly wanted anything but meat.'
Jane, mother of Lucien, 11 months

This stir-fry has just the right shapes for your baby when he's starting out and it's quick to cook – you don't have to marinate the beef if you are in a hurry. (Remember to wash your hands after handling the raw chilli, because chilli juice can sting.)

Serves 2 adults and 1 baby

300g (10½oz) lean beef steak
2 garlic cloves, finely chopped or crushed
3–4cm (1¼–1½in) piece fresh ginger, peeled and finely sliced
¼ red chilli, chopped (deseeded and veins removed) or dried
    chilli flakes, to taste (optional)
3–4 spring onions, finely sliced
1 tbsp fresh coriander, chopped (optional)
1 tbsp sesame oil
6–8 broccoli florets, halved
oil for frying

Cut the beef into thin strips and put them into a large bowl.
  Add the garlic, ginger, chilli, spring onions and half of the coriander (if using). Add the sesame oil and stir well. Cover and leave to marinate for a couple of hours.
  Lightly steam the broccoli. Heat a large pan (preferably a wok) until very hot and add a little oil. Transfer the marinated ingredients to the wok and add the broccoli.
  Stir-fry for 2–3 minutes, keeping the pan very hot all the time.
  Sprinkle with the remaining coriander and serve immediately (cooled for your baby) with noodles or rice, accompanied by green vegetables.

Option

• Adults may prefer this dish with some soy sauce or tamari. Simply take your baby's portion out when the beef and vegetables are cooked and then add the extra sauce to the rest, stirring briefly.

Chunky Chilli Con Carne

This is a real favourite with many families – filling, tasty and easy to make. And it's surprisingly adaptable, even for the early days of BLW when your baby needs large pieces of food to grab. Simply allow the meat to stay in large clumps, rather than breaking them up, and your baby will be able to get hold of them and take them to his mouth. Cutting the onions into wedges will make the pieces easier to grab, too. Go easy on the chilli the first time you make it, until you know how hot your baby likes it. Chilli con carne tastes better if it's kept in the fridge overnight and eaten the next day, so this is worth bearing in mind when you're planning your meals. Be sure to reheat it thoroughly before serving.

Serves 2 adults and 1 baby, generously

oil for frying
2 medium onions, cut into wedges or chopped
250g (9oz) lean minced beef
¼–½ tsp crushed dried chilli flakes (or chilli powder), to taste
1 garlic clove, finely chopped or crushed
½ tsp ground cumin
1 small carrot, grated (optional)
1 celery stick, finely chopped (optional)
400g (14oz) tin tomatoes, chopped
400g (14oz) tin red kidney beans, drained and rinsed (or approx 100g/3½oz dried beans, pre-cooked – see page 51)

Heat the oil in a large pan, add the onions and fry until just beginning to soften. Add the mince to the pan and cook until browned, turning as necessary and allowing the meat to stay in large clumps. Add the chilli flakes, garlic, cumin, carrot and celery (if using) and allow to cook for another minute or two.

Add the tomatoes, stir well and simmer for 35–40 minutes.

Add the kidney beans and stir well. Cook for a further 10 minutes, to allow the beans to heat through.

Serve warm, with rice (or couscous) and a salad. A soured cream dip or guacamole on the side is good too – and you may like to have some cooling natural yoghurt on hand in case you have made it a little too spicy for your baby.

Beef and Onion Stew

'We eat lots of stews – Harry likes to see what he's got and to pick out the bits he wants. He still doesn't like things mixed together too much.'

Alison, mother of Harry, 2 years

Serves 2 adults and 1 baby

oil for frying

2 medium onions, cut into wedges

350g (12½oz) lean braising or stewing beef steak, cut to suit
   your baby

1 medium carrot, cut to suit your baby

450ml (16fl oz) beef or vegetable stock (low-salt or home-made,
   see pages 182–3)

1 bouquet garni

freshly ground black pepper, to taste

approx 1 tbsp cornflour

Heat the oil in a pan and add the onions and beef pieces. Fry gently, turning the meat occasionally until the beef is browned on all sides and the onion is beginning to soften. Add the carrot, stock, bouquet garni and black pepper and bring to the boil. Cover and simmer for 1–2 hours, until the meat is tender.

When you are almost ready to serve the stew, remove the bouquet garni and turn up the heat slightly. Remove 2 tbsp of the stock and mix to a smooth paste with the cornflour. Add a further few tbsp of stock, then return the stock plus cornflour to the pan and cook for 3–5 minutes, stirring gently, until the sauce thickens.

Serve warm with dumplings (see page 152) or bread, potatoes and green vegetables.

Option

• You can add mushrooms, potato, swede or turnip, along with (or instead of) the carrot. Sweet potato, squash and courgette are also good – add them a bit later so they don't disintegrate.

Goulash

This traditional Hungarian dish is based on slow-cooked beef, which is easy for a baby to chew, so it's good for beginners. If you want to include more vegetables you can add sliced carrots, potatoes or parsnips before it goes into the oven.

Serves 2 adults and 1 baby

oil for frying

1 medium onion, cut into wedges

½ green pepper, deseeded and cut to suit your baby

350g (12½oz) lean braising or stewing beef, cut to suit your baby

1–2 tsp paprika

2 tbsp tomato purée

2 tbsp plain flour

pinch of grated nutmeg

pinch of freshly ground black pepper

approx 250ml (9fl oz) beef or vegetable stock (low-salt or home-made, see pages 182–3)

1 large tomato, skinned and roughly chopped

1 bouquet garni

100ml (3½fl oz) soured cream (optional)

1 tbsp fresh parsley or chives, chopped (optional)

Preheat the oven to 160°C/325°F/Gas Mark 3. Heat the oil in a pan, add the onion and pepper and fry until they begin to soften. Add the beef and cook for 3–5 minutes, until browned all over. Add the paprika and cook gently for 1 minute. Stir in the tomato purée, flour, nutmeg and black pepper, and cook for 3 more minutes.

Add half the stock, the tomato and bouquet garni and bring to the boil. Stir until thickened, then add more stock until the sauce is the consistency you want. Transfer the mixture to an ovenproof casserole (with a lid) and oven cook for 1½–2 hours.

Remove the bouquet garni, add a swirl of soured cream (if using), and sprinkle with chopped parsley or chives (if using) before serving. Serve warm with dumplings made with 1 tsp caraway seeds (see page 152), potatoes or rice, and vegetables.

Meat Loaf

Meat loaf is a great dish for baby-led weaning, as it holds together perfectly when cooked and is soft and moist to eat. You can adapt the seasoning to suit your taste, or add a dash of Worcestershire sauce to give it extra flavour.

Serves 2 adults and 1 baby, generously

oil, for greasing
450g (1lb) lean minced beef
100g (3½oz) good-quality sausage meat (or squeeze
    the meat out of your favourite sausages)
1 medium onion, finely chopped
2 tbsp tomato purée (optional)
100g (3½oz) fresh breadcrumbs
1 tsp dried mixed herbs
freshly ground black pepper, to taste
1 medium carrot, grated (optional)
1 celery stick, finely chopped (optional)
1 egg, beaten

Preheat the oven to 180°C/350°F/Gas Mark 4 and lightly grease a 450g (1lb) loaf tin.

Put the beef, sausage meat, onion, tomato purée (if using), breadcrumbs, herbs, black pepper, carrot and celery (if using) into a large bowl and mix well.

Add the egg and mix thoroughly, using your hands to squeeze the mixture (flouring or wetting them first will help to stop it sticking). Transfer the mixture to the loaf tin. Press down well and cover with foil.

Bake in the oven for about 1 hour, or until the loaf begins to come away from the sides of the tin.

Remove from the tin before slicing and serving warm with green vegetables or salad. If you're planning to eat it cold, allow to cool before slicing.

Options

• Use a blender or food processor if you want the meat loaf really smooth.
• Leftovers can be mixed with a tomato-based sauce and served with pasta.

Meatballs in Tomato Sauce

Meatballs are very easy for babies to grip, and nice and soft to eat.

Serves 2 adults and 1 baby

For the meatballs:
500g (1lb 2oz) lean minced beef

1 egg, beaten

2–3 garlic cloves, finely chopped or
   crushed

1 tsp dried mixed herbs or oregano

2 tbsp chopped fresh parsley

1 tbsp balsamic vinegar

25–50g (1–2oz) breadcrumbs
   (1 slice of bread)

oil for frying (if needed)

For the sauce:
1 medium onion finely chopped

1–2 garlic cloves, chopped

1 tbsp tomato purée

400g (14oz) tin chopped tomatoes or
   400ml (14fl oz) passata

1 handful fresh basil leaves, torn

pinch of freshly ground black
   pepper, to taste

Put all the meatball ingredients except the oil into a bowl and combine using your hands (or use a food processor). Shape the mixture into balls the size of golf balls. If you have time, put them in the fridge to firm up for an hour or so.

Heat the oil in a frying pan, add the meatballs and fry gently until they are browned all over, turning as necessary. Lift the meatballs out of the pan with a slotted spoon (to drain off the oil) and set aside. Return the pan to the heat and add the onion. Fry gently for a few minutes, then add the garlic and cook until the onion is soft. Stir in the tomato purée, then add the tomatoes, half the basil and the black pepper. Stir well and bring to the boil. Return the meatballs to the pan, cover and simmer for 10–15 minutes until the sauce has thickened and the meatballs are cooked through (test one by cutting in half – there should be no pink meat).

Serve warm, with pasta, rice or couscous, with the remaining basil sprinkled on top.

Options

- If you like you can replace the tinned tomatoes with 6–8 ripe plum tomatoes (or about 15 cherry tomatoes), blanched, peeled and chopped.
- Try making meatballs from minced lamb or pork, or half-pork, half-beef.
- Adding 1 tbsp of Parmesan cheese to the meatball mixture will give extra flavour.

Shepherd's Pie

This is traditional family comfort food – perfect for cold winter evenings. Your baby will be able to manage this dish once he can open his fist on purpose and no longer needs to have sticks of food poking out. If he's not quite there yet, serve it with sticks of steamed vegetables and let him have some of the shepherd's pie to play with.

Serves 2 adults and 1 baby

450g (1lb) potatoes, peeled and cut into chunks

about 150ml (5fl oz) milk

1 large carrot, sliced

30–40g (1–1½oz) swede, chopped

1 stick of celery, chopped

300ml (11fl oz) lamb or vegetable stock (low-salt or home-made, see pages 182–3)

oil for frying

1 medium onion, finely chopped

300g (10½oz) lean minced lamb

1 tbsp plain flour

1 tbsp tomato purée

splash of Worcestershire sauce (optional)

1 tbsp chopped fresh rosemary or thyme (or 1 tsp dried rosemary or thyme)

80g (3oz) (just over half a mugful) frozen peas

25g (1oz) butter (preferably unsalted)

50g (2oz) cheese, grated (optional)

freshly ground black pepper, to taste

Preheat the oven to 180°C/350°F/Gas Mark 4. Put the potatoes in a pan with enough milk to come almost halfway up the potatoes. Bring to the boil, cover and simmer for 20–30 minutes until soft.

Meanwhile, put the carrot, swede, celery and stock into another pan and bring to the boil. Cover and simmer until the vegetables are just tender, then lift them out with a slotted spoon and set aside, reserving the stock for later.

Heat the oil in a large pan and cook the onion until soft. Add the mince and cook for 3–5 minutes, turning frequently. Break up any clumps as you go (or leave them, to make the meat easier for your baby to grab.)

Stir in the flour, making sure it doesn't form lumps, and gradually add half the stock, stirring constantly. Add the tomato purée and Worcestershire sauce (if using) and stir. Add the vegetables, rosemary or thyme and peas, and mix well.

Bring the mixture to the boil, reduce the heat and simmer gently for 10 minutes. Add more of the stock as the mixture thickens, until you get the consistency you want.

Add the butter to the potatoes and the milk they were cooked in, and mash well. Transfer the meat mixture into an ovenproof dish and spread the mashed potato over the top. Sprinkle with the grated cheese and some black pepper and put the dish into the oven. Bake for 25–30 minutes.

Serve warm, with vegetables.

Option

• Although true shepherd's pie is made with lamb, this recipe also works well with minced beef (called cottage pie). If using beef, replace the rosemary with dried mixed herbs and the lamb stock with home-made or low-salt beef (or vegetable) stock.

Lamb and Mint Sausages

Shop-bought sausages normally need to have their skins removed so that babies can manage them safely. These sausages have no skins, and the shape is perfect for babies starting out. If you have time, put them in the fridge to firm up for an hour or so before you cook them. These are best fried but can also be oven baked.

Serves 2 adults and 1 baby

approx 80g (3oz) peas (just over half a mugful)
½ medium leek, finely chopped
250g (9oz) minced lamb
2 tsp fresh mint, chopped (or 1 tsp dried)
1 tsp dried mixed herbs
freshly ground black pepper, to taste
oil, for frying (optional)

Steam, boil or microwave the peas and leek, then drain. Blend or mash thoroughly, to make a purée. Add the lamb and mix well.

Add the herbs and black pepper and stir well. Shape the mixture into small sausage shapes to suit your baby (flouring or wetting your hands will help to stop it sticking).

Heat a frying pan, with a little oil if needed. Fry the sausages for about 10 minutes, turning occasionally, until cooked through (test one by cutting it in half – there should be no pink meat). Alternatively, put them on a greased baking sheet and bake in the oven at 220°C/425°F/Gas Mark 7 for about 25 minutes.

Lamb Tagine

This Moroccan dish is traditionally cooked slowly on the hob in a special pot called a tagine, but a covered pan or casserole will do. Alternatively, you can use the oven (or a slow cooker). The sweetness of the apricots with the tender lamb and rich mix of spices will give your baby a delicious new range of tastes to discover.

Don't be put off if you don't have all the spices listed below – you'll still be able to make a tasty dish with a combination of those you do have.

Serves 2 adults and 1 baby

oil for frying
1 medium onion, cut into wedges or finely chopped
2 garlic cloves, finely chopped or crushed
3–4cm (1¼–1½in) piece of fresh ginger, peeled and grated or chopped
300g (10½oz) lean lamb meat, cut into strips
1 tsp paprika
1 tsp turmeric
1 tsp ground cinnamon
1 tsp coriander seeds, crushed

¼ tsp cayenne pepper
pinch of saffron (optional)
pinch of freshly ground black pepper
2–3 medium tomatoes, roughly chopped (or ½ x 400g/14oz tin tomatoes, drained and chopped)
6–8 dried apricots or prunes
1 tbsp sultanas or raisins
approx 200ml (7fl oz) lamb or vegetable stock (low-salt or home-made, see pages 182–3)
1 tbsp chopped fresh coriander (optional)

Preheat the oven to 160°C/325°F/Gas Mark 3. Heat the oil (preferably in a flame-proof casserole so you don't have to transfer the food at the next stage) and add the onion. Fry gently until soft. Add the garlic and ginger, and cook for another minute or two. Add the lamb and continue frying gently until the pieces are browned on all sides.

Mix together all the dried spices and the black pepper, and add them to the pan. Fry for a couple of minutes. Add the tomatoes and dried fruit and heat through.

Put a lid on the casserole (or transfer the ingredients from the pan to a casserole) and add enough stock to almost cover the other ingredients. Put the casserole in the oven and cook for about 2 hours, giving it a stir about halfway through.

Sprinkle with fresh coriander (if using) before serving, warm, with plain couscous or rice (with a squeeze of lemon or lime juice) and steamed green beans or salad.

Spicy Lamb Patties

These delicious patties melt in the mouth – perfect for babies who are just starting out. If you don't have time to prepare the cardamom pods and cloves, you can add 2 tsp ready-ground cardamom and 1 tsp ground cloves instead.

Serves 2 adults and 1 baby

12–15 cardamom pods
8 cloves
500g (1lb 2oz) lean minced lamb
**4–5cm (1¾–2in) piece of fresh ginger, peeled and grated or
    finely chopped**
½ tsp turmeric
½ tsp ground cumin
approx ½ tsp chilli powder, according to taste (optional)
30–50g (1–2oz) breadcrumbs (1 slice of bread)
1 egg, beaten
2 tbsp thick (Greek-style) natural yoghurt
oil for frying (optional)

Use a knife to split open the cardamom pods and put the seeds into a mortar with the cloves (discard the pods). Grind to a powder. (This can also be done using an electric grinder.)

Transfer the powder to a large bowl and add all the remaining ingredients except the egg, yoghurt and oil. Mix well. Add the egg and yoghurt and mix thoroughly, so that everything is bound together.

Shape the mixture into small patties (flouring or wetting your hands will help to stop it sticking), making sure they are all roughly the same thickness. If you have time, cover them and put them in the fridge to firm up for an hour or so.

Heat a frying pan, and add a little oil, if needed. Fry the patties for 5–10 minutes on each side, until cooked through and browned.

Serve warm, with salad, couscous and roasted vegetables, or rice.

Toad-in-the-Hole

Toad-in-the-Hole is a traditional favourite for many families.

Serves 2 adults and 1 baby, generously

125g (4½oz) plain flour
pinch of freshly ground black pepper (optional)
1–2 eggs (2 make a richer batter)
300ml (11fl oz) milk (or half-water, half-milk)
3 tbsp olive oil
6–8 good-quality medium or small sausages (preferably herby)

Put the flour into a mixing bowl and add the black pepper (if using). Make a well in the centre and break the egg(s) into it. Pour in half the milk (or the milk and water mixture). Beat or whisk the ingredients together, starting in the middle and gradually working in the flour.

Gradually add the rest of the liquid and continue beating until any remaining lumps have disappeared. The consistency should be like single cream (or double cream, if you have used 2 eggs). Put the mixture in the fridge to rest for at least 15 minutes. Meanwhile, preheat the oven to 220°C/425°F/Gas Mark 7.

Pour the olive oil into a shallow roasting tin (approx 20 x 28cm/8 x 11in, 4cm/1½in deep) and put it in the oven until the oil is smoking hot.

Arrange the sausages in the tin, evenly spaced, and pour the batter around them.

Return the tin to the oven and bake for 25–30 minutes, until the batter is risen and golden. (Don't be tempted to open the oven door in the early stages as it could make the batter collapse.)

Toad-in-the-Hole is best eaten straight from the oven (cooled for your baby). Remove sausage skins from your baby's portion and serve with vegetables of your choice, preferably steamed.

Option

• Add up to 1 tbsp of mustard to the batter mixture to give it an extra kick.

Tip: Cutting your baby's sausage in half lengthways once cooked will help it to cool more quickly and make it easier for him to pick up.

Classic Roast Dinner

Roast dinners – with plenty of vegetables and home-made gravy – are classic family meals. Served with Yorkshire puddings (see page 105) and horseradish sauce (with beef), apple sauce (with pork), mint sauce (with lamb) or stuffing (with chicken), a roast dinner will give your baby plenty of flavours to try.

Potatoes and vegetables, such as sweet potato, carrots and parsnips, can be roasted (see page 150) with the meat; other vegetables, stuffings, sauces, gravy and Yorkshire puddings can be cooked while the meat is 'resting'.

Serves 2 adults and 1 baby, generously

**1 joint of meat, about 1kg (2lb 3oz), more if on the bone, or 1
    small chicken (preferably organic)**
potatoes for roasting (optional)
2 whole bulbs garlic (unpeeled), cut in half
approx 2 tbsp oil (less if the meat has a good covering of fat)
a little freshly ground black pepper
for beef: **a small bunch of fresh thyme, rosemary, bay and/or sage**
for pork: **a small bunch of fresh thyme, rosemary and/or sage**
for lamb: **a small bunch of fresh rosemary and/or mint**
for chicken: **2 unwaxed lemons, halved; 50g (2oz) butter
    (preferably unsalted) or 2–3 tbsp oil; a small bunch of
    fresh rosemary and 6 bay leaves**

Take the meat out of the fridge half an hour before you want to cook it.

For chicken, check there is no bag of giblets in the cavity. If you want to stuff it (see page 105), do this now. Alternatively, pierce two of the lemon halves several times with a knife and put them inside the cavity, together with one of the bay leaves, a few springs of the rosemary and half a bulb of garlic. Rub butter or oil all over the breast and legs.

For crispy crackling on pork, use a sharp knife to score the skin deeply into narrow strips, then rub it with oil.

If the cooking time isn't on the packaging, weigh the meat (including stuffing, if any) and calculate how long you need to cook it for (see overleaf). Preheat the oven to at least 190°C/375°F/Gas Mark 5.

If roasting potatoes, put them into the roasting tin with the (remaining) garlic and herbs (and, for chicken, the other lemon halves) and coat them with a thin layer of the oil. Put the meat in the middle of the tin, keeping the fatty or buttered side up, and add black pepper. Cover the tin with foil and put it into the centre of the oven. Leave to cook for the recommended time. Meanwhile, you can prepare any vegetables for steaming or boiling or make your Yorkshire pudding batter and stuffing mix (if serving separately).

About 30 minutes before the end of the cooking time, remove the foil. Baste the meat and the potatoes with the hot fat from the roasting tin.

Tips: If the cooking time of the meat is longer than 1½ hours, put the potatoes in the oven a little later, so they don't overcook.

You can use leftover meat in dishes such as curries, rissoles, salads and soups. Any bones can be used for meat stock (see page 182–3).

To check the meat is cooked, push a skewer into the thickest part (for chicken, this is the thigh) and check the juice that runs out. For pork and chicken, the juices should be completely clear; lamb and beef can safely be eaten slightly 'rare' in the middle, so the juices may appear pink, but not red. *If in doubt, cook it for a bit longer.* (You may need to take out the roast potatoes so they don't burn.)

When the meat is cooked, lift it out of the tin (discarding the garlic), and put it on to a chopping board or carving dish. Cover with foil and a tea towel and let it 'rest' for 30 minutes (to make it tender and easy to carve). Meanwhile return the potatoes to the bottom of the oven, cook any Yorkshire puddings, stuffing (if separate) and/or other vegetables, and use the juices from the roasting tin to make 'real' gravy (see page 106). Aim for everything to be ready when the meat has finished resting.

Oven roasting times for meat

Type of meat	Oven temperature (°C/°F/Gas Mark)	Minutes per 500g (1lb 2oz)	Plus additional minutes
Beef or lamb	190–220/375–425/5–7	25–30	25
Pork	190–220/375–425/5–7	30–35	30
Chicken	190–200/375–400/5–6	20	20

Note: The 'additional minutes' in the last column are to give the heat time to reach the meat and kick-start the cooking process. Meat must be completely unfrozen before it is cooked, to prevent food poisoning. If in doubt, cook it for longer than usual on a slow heat.

To make a simple stuffing ...

250g (9oz) good quality pork sausage meat

1 small onion, finely chopped

125g (4½oz) fresh breadcrumbs

1 egg, beaten

1 tbsp fresh sage, chopped (or 1 tsp dried)

freshly ground black pepper, to taste

Combine all the ingredients and mix well with a fork (or food processor).

Either use to stuff a chicken (before cooking), by pushing the mixture loosely into the large opening, or shape the mixture into balls, place them on a small, lightly greased roasting tin and cook them in the oven for about 30 minutes.

To make Yorkshire puddings ...

Makes approximately 12 puddings

125g (4½oz) plain flour

2 medium eggs or 1 large egg

300ml (10fl oz) milk (or milk with a little water, for lighter puddings)

oil for cooking

> **Tip:** *This batter recipe can also be used for Toad-in-the-Hole (see page 102) or to make rich pancakes (see page 63). You can keep it in the fridge for a couple of days; if it thickens, just stir in a little extra milk or water.*

Preheat the oven to 220°C/425°F/Gas Mark 7. Sift the flour into a bowl and make a well in the centre. Break the eggs into the flour and add half the milk.

Beat or whisk the ingredients together vigorously. Gradually add the rest of the liquid and continue beating until all lumps have disappeared. Put the batter into the fridge for 20–30 minutes.

Put a little oil into each section of a muffin or Yorkshire pudding tin and heat in the oven until smoking hot.

Beat the batter mixture again and pour 1–2 tbsp into each well (don't fill them – the puddings will expand considerably during cooking). Put the tin in the top of the oven and bake for 10–15 minutes until the puddings are puffy and golden brown. Don't open the oven door too soon or they'll sink!

Serve straight from the oven.

To make real gravy ...

This is just the best gravy to serve with a meat roast – and much more tasty than gravy made with commercial gravy granules, which contain a lot of salt. The quantities of ingredients, and the amount of gravy made, will depend on how much meat juice there is and how thick you like your gravy.

> **the juices from the roasting tin in which the meat has cooked**
> **a few tbsp plain flour**
> **hot low-salt or home-made meat or vegetable stock (see pages**
> **182–3, or if you have boiled your vegetables – other than**
> **potatoes – use that water)**

Remove the meat from the roasting tin; scoop off the fatty layer from the meat juices and discard. Then scrape the bottom of the tin to loosen all the caramelised bits and put the tin on the hob.

Over a low heat, add a little flour and stir it into the meat juices. Keep adding small amounts of flour until you get a thick paste. Keep cooking and stirring for 2–3 minutes until the mixture turns brown.

Add up to 100ml (3½fl oz) stock, a little at a time, blending it with the paste as you go.

Keep the mixture just about at boiling point, and keep stirring as it thickens. When it has finished thickening, add more stock until you get the consistency you want. Continue cooking for another 1–2 minutes, then serve.

Tip: *If you have roasted vegetables separately, include the juices and caramelised bits from that tin, too.*

MAINS: POULTRY

Chicken is an easy meat to prepare for babies and even those just starting out can usually eat it successfully, in strips or on the bone. Breast meat can be a little dry, so recipes that keep the meat moist are ideal at first. Most babies enjoy chicken drumsticks – but remember to remove gristle and splint bones first.

Lemon and Tarragon Chicken

This light chicken dish will give your baby the chance to discover the distinctive flavour of tarragon. It's a good dish for beginners because the chicken strips are easy to pick up.

Serves 2 adults and 1 baby

2–3 chicken breasts, cut into strips
2 tbsp fresh lemon juice
1 tbsp fresh tarragon (or 1 tsp dried)
2 tbsp double cream
freshly ground black pepper, to taste

Put the chicken and lemon juice in a pan and heat until the juice is just boiling, then turn down the heat, cover, and simmer gently for about 10 minutes until the chicken is cooked. Add a little water, if necessary, to prevent the pan boiling dry.

Add the tarragon, cream and black pepper, and stir until the cream is warmed through.

Serve warm with rice, pasta or couscous and steamed vegetables.

107

Green Thai Curried Chicken and Rice

This is a quick and easy recipe to make. Chicken breast strips are good for a baby who is just beginning BLW to chomp on, and the peas are great fun for babies practising their pincer grip.

This recipe uses a mild, home-made Thai green curry paste. If you use shop-bought paste (which is likely to be hotter), reduce the amount stated in this recipe and taste the finished dish before offering it to your baby.

Serves 2 adults and 1 baby

approx 2 tbsp mild Thai Green Curry Paste (see page 186), to taste

2–3 chicken breasts, sliced to suit your baby

400g (14oz) tin coconut milk

200g (7oz) rice (about ¾ of a mugful)

1–2 handfuls frozen peas and/or green beans

Heat a large saucepan or wok on the hob and add the Thai curry paste.

Add the chicken and fry briefly, until the outside of the chicken pieces is sealed. Add the coconut milk, bring to the boil, then reduce the heat and simmer for about 15 minutes.

Meanwhile, start cooking the rice so that it will be almost ready as the vegetables are becoming soft (the exact time needed will depend on the type of rice you use – but don't overcook it).

Add the frozen peas or beans to the curry and cook for a further 4–5 minutes (beans may need a little longer – about 6 minutes).

Drain the rice and add it to the chicken and vegetables and stir. Cook for a further 2–3 minutes to allow the rice to absorb some of the sauce.

Serve warm, on its own or with a salad.

Options

- A sliced red or yellow pepper will give added colour and flavour.
- The green beans can be broken into smaller pieces if your baby can manage them.
- You may prefer to replace the rice with noodles.

Tomato Chicken

This is a delicious, warmly spiced dish that a baby starting out will be able to manage easily. It also works well with chicken thighs or drumsticks but may take longer to cook.

Serves 2 adults and 1 baby

oil for frying
1 medium onion, chopped or cut into wedges
1 tsp ground cumin
2 tsp ground coriander
2–3 chicken breasts, cut into strips
400g (14oz) tin tomatoes, chopped
1 tbsp tomato purée
1 tbsp chopped fresh coriander (optional)

Heat the oil in a pan, add the onion and fry for a few minutes until soft.

Add the cumin and coriander and cook for 2–3 minutes, then add the chicken and cook until lightly browned on all sides (but not cooked through).

Add the tomatoes and tomato purée. Bring to the boil, cover and simmer for about 20 minutes, until the chicken is thoroughly cooked.

Sprinkle with the fresh coriander before serving, warm, with rice and vegetables of your choice.

Option

• Try adding a little chilli powder if you and your baby like spicy food.

Moroccan Chicken

This is a tasty introduction to Moroccan flavours. Babies just starting out will be able to manage the courgette and chicken; older babies will be able to get hold of the chickpeas, too.

Serves 2 adults and 1 baby

oil for frying
1 medium onion, finely chopped
1–2 tsp ground cumin
½ tsp ground cinnamon
3 chicken thighs
250ml (9fl oz) chicken or vegetable stock (low-salt or
   home-made – see pages 182–3)
pinch of chilli (or more depending on your preference), to taste
1–2 tbsp roughly chopped fresh coriander
1 large courgette, cut into sticks
¾ x 400g (14oz) tin chickpeas, rinsed and drained (or approx
   75g/2½oz dried chickpeas, pre-cooked – see page 51)
1–2 tbsp chopped fresh parsley
juice of 1 lemon (approx 4 tbsp)
freshly ground black pepper, to taste

Heat the oil in a pan, add the onion and fry for a few minutes until soft.

Add the cumin and cinnamon and cook for 2–3 minutes. Add the chicken thighs, stock, chilli and coriander, and bring to the boil. Cover and simmer for 25 minutes.

Add the courgette and chickpeas, bring back to the boil and simmer for a further 10–20 minutes, until the courgettes are soft.

Stir in the parsley and the lemon juice. Add black pepper to taste and serve warm with couscous, rice or quinoa. Cut the chicken into strips for your baby.

Option

• If you prefer a sweeter dish, and your baby is over a year old, you can add 1 tbsp of clear honey with the oil, herbs and spices.

Turkey and Vegetable Burgers

These burgers are good warm or cold, with home-made Spicy Tomato Salsa (see page 154). If you can't find turkey already minced, you can buy turkey breasts and mince them yourself, using a food processor or mincer. If you have time, put the burgers in the fridge to firm up for an hour or so before you cook them.

Serves 2 adults and 1 baby, generously

1 small parsnip, chopped
½ medium leek, finely chopped
250g (9oz) minced turkey
2 tsp fresh sage, chopped (or 1 tsp dried)
1 tsp dried mixed herbs
freshly ground black pepper, to taste

Preheat the oven to 220°C/425°F/Gas Mark 7 and lightly grease a baking sheet.

Steam, boil or microwave the parsnip and leek, then drain. Blend or mash thoroughly, to make a purée. Add the turkey and mix well. Add the herbs and black pepper and stir thoroughly.

Shape the mixture into about 8 burgers approx 1cm (½in) thick (flouring or wetting your hands will help to stop it sticking), pressing them together and making sure they are all roughly the same thickness.

Bake in the oven for about 25 minutes until cooked through (remove one and test it by cutting it in half – there should be no pink meat).

Serve warm, with new potatoes or couscous, and vegetables.

Options

• If you prefer, you can cook the burgers in a frying pan, turning them once so that they brown on both sides. They also work well shaped into sausages.
• You can make similar burgers using pork instead of turkey and replacing the parsnip with 1 small apple (peeled, cored and chopped) and 2 sticks of celery (chopped).

Chicken Stir-Fry with Noodles

This stir-fry is colourful and the shapes are fun for small hands to grasp. Cut the vegetables very thinly so they are not too crunchy for your baby.

Serves 2 adults and 1 baby

100–150g (3½–5½oz) noodles

2 tbsp oil

approx 2 tsp sesame oil

2 medium carrots, peeled and cut into thin strips

4 whole baby sweetcorn, quartered lengthways

1 red pepper, deseeded and cut into thin strips

1 yellow pepper, deseeded and cut into thin strips

1 garlic clove, finely chopped or crushed

1 celery stalk, strings removed, cut into very thin strips

2 chicken breasts, cut into strips

Cook the noodles according to the instructions on the packet, then drain and return to the pan. Add a little of the oil and toss the noodles in it, then cover and set aside.

Heat a wok or a deep, non-stick frying pan and add a little sesame oil. Stir-fry the carrots, baby sweetcorn and peppers for 30 seconds.

Add the garlic and celery and stir-fry for a further 30 seconds, then lift the vegetables out of the pan (draining off the oil) and set aside.

Heat some more of the sesame oil in the pan, if necessary, then add the chicken strips. Stir-fry for about 3 minutes, until the chicken is cooked through. Add the cooked vegetables and noodles and stir-fry for 1 minute.

Serve warm with, for the adults, a dash of soy sauce or tamari.

Options

- You can also add mushrooms, spring onions, pak choi, finely sliced broccoli or green beans, mangetout or fresh sliced ginger to this dish. Toasted sesame seeds can be added just before serving; cashew nuts are also tasty, for children over five and adults.
- You can leave out the noodles and serve the stir-fry with rice instead.

MAINS: FISH

Fish is simple to prepare, quick to cook and very nutritious. It can be grilled, fried, oven-baked or stir-fried, or made into fishcakes or fish pie, and the texture is easy for babies to eat. Just watch out for any bones, even if the fish has already been filleted.

Grilled Salmon

This is proper fast food – a simple, nutritious dish that takes just 10 minutes to cook. If you serve it with couscous and salad you can have the whole thing on the table in less than 15 minutes. Most fish, including mackerel, can be cooked this way.

Serves 2 adults and 1 baby

2 salmon fillets
oil or butter (preferably unsalted)

Preheat the grill to Medium. Put the salmon fillets on the grill tray and brush them with the oil or butter. Grill for about 10 minutes, or until cooked through.

Serve warm, with rice, couscous, new or mashed potatoes, and vegetables or salad and a squeeze of lemon. Spicy Tomato Salsa (see page 154) is also good with grilled fish. Check carefully to make sure there are no bones in your baby's portion.

Fish 'n' Chips

Home-cooked fish and chips can be just as delicious as the take-away version – and much better for you.

Serves 2 adults and 1 baby

450g (1lb) potatoes (2–3 large ones)
oil for greasing and coating the potatoes
2 large plaice fillets (or other white fish)
1 egg
25–50g (1–2oz) breadcrumbs (preferably stale, dried or
   toasted)
freshly ground black pepper, to taste
oil for frying

Cut the potatoes into wedges (skins on) or chip shapes and put into a pan of cold water. Preheat the oven to 190°C/375°F/Gas Mark 5.

Put enough oil into a small roasting tin to just cover the bottom and heat it (on the hob is fine).

Dry the wedges with a clean tea towel, add to the hot oil and shake the tin to coat them. Put the tin in the oven and bake for about 20 minutes.

Meanwhile, pat the fish on both sides with kitchen paper to dry it.

Beat the egg in a shallow dish and put the breadcrumbs into another one, with a little black pepper.

Dip each fillet into the beaten egg so it is covered on all sides, then press it into the breadcrumbs on both sides, so that it is evenly coated.

Heat the oil in a frying pan and add the fish. Fry gently for about 5 minutes on each side, until the fish is cooked through and the coating is brown and crispy.

Serve the fish with a squeeze of lemon juice, with the potato wedges and some vegetables alongside. Check carefully to make sure there are no bones in your baby's portion.

Option

• You can use sweet potatoes instead of, or as well as, ordinary potatoes.

Baked Salmon and Pesto Parcels

Salmon is an easy fish for babies to eat, as it holds together well when cooked.

Serves 2 adults and 1 baby

2 salmon fillets
1 tbsp fresh pesto (see pages 184–5)

Preheat the oven to 190°C/375°F/Gas Mark 5. Place each salmon fillet in the centre of a piece of lightly greased aluminium foil (large enough to seal by scrunching together). Spread the pesto over the fish. Close the foil over the top of each fillet and scrunch together to make a loose parcel.
   Place the wrapped fillets on a baking sheet and put them in the oven.
   Bake for about 15 minutes, or until the fish is cooked through.
Serve warm, with rice or new potatoes and steamed vegetables or salad. Check carefully to make sure there are no bones in your baby's portion.

Options

- The same method can be used to make lemon and herb fish parcels. Just swap the pesto for a little butter, a squeeze of lemon juice and some chopped dill, parsley or basil.
- If you find the foil parcels too fiddly (or you don't have any foil), you can cook the fillets together in a covered ovenproof dish.

Salmon and Broccoli Bake

This comforting bake is nicely balanced in terms of nutrition; with fish, vegetables, pasta, herbs and dairy foods. For a quicker way to make the sauce, see page 188.

Serves 2 adults and 1 baby, generously

250g (9oz) pasta shapes

1 medium head broccoli, cut into large florets

25g (1oz) butter (preferably unsalted)

25g (1oz) plain flour

600ml (1 pint) milk

2 tbsp chopped fresh parsley (optional)

1 tbsp chopped fresh dill (optional)

3 skinless salmon fillets, cut into large chunks

50–75g (2–2½oz) cheese, grated, (or enough for topping)

25–40g (1–1½oz) breadcrumbs, stale or toasted (optional)

Cook the pasta in a pan of boiling water for slightly less than the time indicated on the packet (so that it's 'al dente'), then drain.

Steam or boil the broccoli until it is just starting to soften, then drain.

Preheat the oven to 180°C/350°F/Gas Mark 4. To make the sauce, melt the butter in a pan and stir in the flour. Cook gently until the mixture starts to bubble. Remove the pan from the heat and gradually add the milk, stirring constantly. Return the pan to the heat and bring to the boil, still stirring. Simmer until thickened, stirring all the time. Stir in the parsley and dill.

Arrange the salmon chunks in an ovenproof dish and add the pasta and broccoli. Pour on the sauce. Mix the cheese with the breadcrumbs, then sprinkle over the surface. Bake in the oven for 30 minutes.

Serve warm with vegetables – steamed baby carrots and green beans or asparagus go particularly well with this dish. Check carefully to make sure there are no bones in your baby's portion.

Fish Cakes

Fish cakes are easy for babies to grab and eat, even when they're just starting out.

Serves 2 adults and 1 baby

a little milk (or water) for poaching
250g (9oz) white fish or salmon fillets
approx 250g (9oz) cooked potatoes (without skins)
knob of butter (preferably unsalted) for mashing potatoes
   (optional)
1 tbsp chopped fresh coriander or parsley
zest of 1 unwaxed lemon (optional)
freshly ground black pepper, to taste
1 egg, beaten
25–50g (1–2oz) breadcrumbs, stale, dried or toasted
oil for frying

Pour some milk into a shallow pan (with lid), to a depth of about ½cm (¼in), and add the fish. Heat until the milk is just beginning to boil, then turn the heat down, cover and simmer for about 5 minutes, until the fish is opaque and cooked in the centre. Drain the fish thoroughly, then skin and flake it, removing any bones.

   Mash the potatoes with the butter, herbs, lemon zest and black pepper. Stir in the flaked fish with a little of the beaten egg.

   Put the remainder of the egg in a shallow dish and put the breadcrumbs into another one. Flour your hands, then take small amounts of the mixture and shape into 4–5 fishcakes. Dip each fishcake into the beaten egg so it is covered on all sides then roll it in the breadcrumbs, so that it is evenly coated.

   Heat the oil in a large frying pan and add the fishcakes. Cook for about 5 minutes on each side, until golden brown. Serve warm, with roasted sweet potato wedges, steamed peas and sweetcorn or baked beans, or with a salad.

Option

• Tinned salmon or tuna (in spring water or oil, not brine) can be used in place of fresh fish. A few chopped spring onions added to the mixture is delicious.

Fish Fingers

These fish fingers can be made into exactly the right size and shape for your baby and the coating is softer and less crunchy than a traditional breadcrumb coating. Perfect for baby-led weaning beginners.

'Chloe really loved home-made fish fingers, even when she was just starting out. They are the perfect shape for babies – really easy to eat and tasty.'
Jo-Ellen, mother of Chloe, 17 months

Serves 2 adults and 1 baby

300g (10½oz) white fish fillet, (e.g. pollack, cod, haddock)
1 egg
50g (2oz) plain flour
50g (2oz) polenta (sometimes labelled coarsely ground
cornmeal or maize flour – not ready-made polenta)
oil or butter (preferably unsalted) for frying

Slice the fish into chunky fingers, making sure there are no bones.

Beat the egg in a shallow dish and mix together the flour and polenta in another dish. Dip each fish finger into the beaten egg so it is covered on all sides, then roll it in the flour and polenta mix so that it is evenly coated.

Heat the oil or butter in a pan. Fry the fish fingers in the hot oil or butter, turning as necessary, until they are brown and crispy on at least two sides.

Serve warm, with new potatoes and steamed vegetables, or a salad.

Fish Pie

Although fish pie won't be an easy food for your baby to eat when he first starts out, he'll soon be able to manage it. Until then he'll have fun licking it off his fingers.

Serves 2 adults and 1 baby

400g (14oz) potatoes
300g (10½oz) white fish fillet (e.g. pollack, cod, haddock)
175ml (6fl oz) milk
1½ tbsp butter (preferably unsalted)
1½ tbsp plain flour
1 tbsp fresh parsley, chopped (optional)
pinch of freshly ground black pepper (optional)
approx 50g (2oz) cheese, grated

Put the potatoes on to boil. Simmer the fish in a saucepan with 100ml of the milk for about 10 minutes until opaque, then lift out with a slotted spoon, reserving the milk. Break the fish up into flakes – discarding any skin and bones – and set aside.

When the potatoes are soft (about 25 minutes), drain and mash them with about 1½ tbsp of the uncooked milk and 1 tsp of the butter, until smooth and creamy.

Preheat the oven to 200°C/400°F/Gas Mark 6. To make the sauce, melt the remaining butter in a pan and stir in the flour. Cook gently until the mixture starts to bubble. Remove the pan from the heat and gradually add the milk used for poaching the fish, followed by the remainder of the milk, stirring constantly to prevent lumps forming. Return the pan to the heat and bring to the boil, still stirring. Reduce the heat and simmer until thickened, stirring all the time.

Remove the sauce from the heat and stir in the flaked fish, parsley and black pepper (if using). Pour the mixture into an ovenproof dish, spread the mashed potatoes on top, then cover with the grated cheese.

Oven bake for 20–30 minutes, until the surface is golden. Serve warm, with a selection of vegetables or a salad.

Option

• Try adding some pre-cooked leeks, green beans or sweetcorn to the fish mixture, or mash some cooked swede, parsnip or carrot with the potato.

Smoked Mackerel Pasta

This delicious, simple dish is perfect for a baby who is learning to pick up slippery things but still needs some stick shapes that he can grip easily. If you break the mackerel into fairly big chunks, he'll be able to get hold of them too. Smoked mackerel is quite salty, so don't give your baby too much of it.

Serves 2 adults and 1 baby

4–6 small broccoli florets

4–6 runner beans, with 'strings' removed and sliced to suit
   your baby

2–3 fillets of smoked mackerel, skinned

oil or butter (preferably unsalted) for frying

1 garlic clove, sliced or chopped

1 tsp chopped fresh oregano

6–8 fresh basil leaves

30–40g (1–1½oz) butter (preferably unsalted)

225g (8oz) pasta shapes

25–50g (1–2oz) Parmesan cheese, grated (optional)

Steam or boil the broccoli and runner beans until tender, then drain.

Break the mackerel into chunks, making sure there are no bones.

Heat the oil or butter in a pan, add the garlic and fry gently for 1–2 minutes. Remove the pan from the heat, lift out the garlic and set aside. While off the heat, add the oregano and basil to the pan, and stir in the butter. Add the steamed broccoli, beans and mackerel, and stir well. Return the pan to a low heat, add the garlic and warm the mixture through gently.

Cook the pasta in a pan of boiling water according to the instructions on the packet until just soft, then drain. Divide the pasta among individual plates with the fish mix on top, and sprinkle with Parmesan cheese (if using), to taste.

Serve warm on its own or with a side salad.

Thai Green Fish Curry

Although Thai curries can be fairly hot, if you use our mild Thai Green Curry Paste (see page 186), this will be a good curry for your baby to try. If you make it with shop-bought curry paste, reduce the amount stated in this recipe and taste the finished dish before offering it to your baby for the first time.

Serves 2 adults and 1 baby

200g (7oz) block of creamed coconut, cut into chunks

300ml (11fl oz) hot water

450g (1lb) thick white fish fillets (e.g. cod, coley, haddock, monkfish)

oil for frying

1–2 garlic cloves, finely chopped or crushed (optional)

1–2 tbsp Thai Green Curry Paste (see page 186), to taste

4–6 green beans, trimmed

4 lime leaves or 2 slices of fresh lime

3–4 cherry tomatoes (optional)

4–5 fresh coriander leaves, chopped

6–8 fresh basil leaves, chopped

Dissolve the chunks of creamed coconut in the hot water.

Cut the fish into thick chunks or short fingers to suit your baby, making sure there are no bones.

Heat the oil in a pan and add the garlic. Fry gently for a minute or two.

Add the coconut mixture to the pan (take care – it may splash). Bring to the boil very gently, stirring constantly, then add the curry paste. Simmer gently and add the fish, green beans and lime leaves/slices.

Simmer gently for 9–10 minutes, then add the tomatoes (if using) and cook for a further 2–3 minutes, until the fish is cooked.

Sprinkle with coriander and basil leaves and serve with plain or sticky rice.

MAINS: EGGS & CHEESE

Eggs and cheese are versatile and nutritious and, because they keep well, they make good 'store-cupboard' meals. However, cheese is quite salty so be sure to serve with plenty of vegetables.

Potato, Leek and Cheese Bake

This simple dish is easy to make and very tasty. See page 188 for an alternative way to make the sauce.

Serves 2 adults and 1 baby

450g (1lb) potatoes (2–3 large ones), cut into fairly thick slices
oil or butter (preferably unsalted) for frying
1 medium leek, washed and cut into chunks
25g (1oz) butter (preferably unsalted)
25g (1oz) plain flour
250ml (9fl oz) milk
75–100g (2½–3½oz) cheese, grated

Steam or boil the potatoes until just cooked and allow to cool.

Heat the oil or butter in a saucepan, add the leek and fry gently until soft.

Preheat the oven to 180°C/350°F/Gas Mark 4. Melt the butter in a pan and stir in the flour. Cook gently for 2–3 minutes until the mixture starts to bubble. Remove the pan from the heat and gradually add the milk, stirring constantly. Return the pan to the heat and bring to the boil, still stirring. Keep stirring the sauce at boiling point until thickened. Remove from the heat and stir in almost all the cheese.

Layer the potatoes over the bottom of an ovenproof dish. Spread the leek on top and pour on the cheese sauce. Sprinkle the remaining cheese on top.

Bake for about 20 minutes, until the surface is golden.

Homity Pie

This traditional pie is delicious; serve it with sticks of vegetables if your baby is just starting out.

Makes 1 large pie or 6 individual pies

250g (9oz) shortcrust pastry, home-made (see page 181) or
   shop-bought, or 1 pre-baked pastry case (or, for individual
   pies, 300g/10½oz pastry)
350g (12½oz) potatoes
oil or butter (preferably unsalted) for frying
450g (1lb) onions, chopped
25g (1oz) butter (preferably unsalted)
1–2 garlic cloves, finely chopped or crushed
2 tsp chopped fresh parsley
pinch of dried thyme
pinch of freshly ground black pepper
1 tbsp milk
100g (3½oz) cheese, grated

To prepare your pastry case, either line a 23cm (9in) pie tin (or six 10cm/4in tins) with pastry (and bake 'blind' if you like – see pages 181–2) or use a ready-made pastry case.

Steam or boil the potatoes until just cooked and allow to cool (or use previously boiled potatoes).

Preheat the oven to 220°C/425°F/Gas Mark 7. Heat the oil or butter in a pan, add the onions and fry gently until soft.

Meanwhile, slice or chop the potatoes and put them into a large bowl. Add the onions, butter, garlic, herbs, black pepper, milk and half the cheese, and mix well.

Transfer the mixed ingredients to the pastry case and sprinkle the remaining cheese on top. Oven bake for 20–25 minutes until golden brown.

Serve warm, with a selection of vegetables.

Options

• Try replacing 250g (9oz) of the onions with leeks, washed and cut into chunks.
• Mix some breadcrumbs with the cheese sprinkled on top, for a slightly crunchy crust.

Simple Broccoli Quiche

This tasty quiche is traditionally made with Gruyère cheese, but Cheddar works too.

Makes 1 large quiche or 6 individual quiches

1 medium head broccoli (florets only)

**250g (9oz) shortcrust pastry (see page 181),
or 1 pre-baked pastry case (or, for individual
pies, 300g/10½oz pastry)**

1 small onion, finely sliced

50–100g (2–3½oz) grated cheese (according to taste)

3 eggs

115ml (4fl oz) milk

pinch of freshly ground black pepper

> **Storage:** *Quiches are easy to cook in batches, for freezing. They can be kept for 2–3 days in the fridge.*

Preheat the oven to 190°C/375°F/Gas Mark 5. Cut the broccoli into small florets and steam or boil for about 2 minutes until just tender, then drain.

To prepare your pastry case, either line a 23cm (9in) pie tin (or six 10cm/4in tins) with pastry (and bake 'blind' if you like – see pages 181–2) or use a ready-made pastry case. Spread the onion in the bottom of the pastry case, add the broccoli and sprinkle half of the cheese over it.

Beat together the eggs and milk and add the black pepper. Pour the egg mixture over the onion, broccoli and cheese, then sprinkle the remaining cheese on top. (The egg mixture should come at least three-quarters of the way up the pastry case. If it doesn't, add another egg, beaten with about 2 tbsp milk.)

Bake in the oven for 40–50 minutes, until the egg is cooked through (test it with a skewer) and the pastry is golden brown.

Serve warm, sliced or in fingers, with new potatoes and either salad, green beans or asparagus for a main meal, or eat it cold for a light lunch.

Options

- Alternative fillings include: a few rashers of grilled bacon, chopped; a little ham, cut into strips; sliced tomatoes, or halved cherry tomatoes; sliced mushrooms; shredded spinach; chopped asparagus.
- For a really rich quiche, replace some of the milk with single cream.
- For a more cheesy quiche, use cheese pastry (see page 181).

Lentil Quiche

This makes a heartier than usual quiche that is rich in nutrients and very tasty. Serve it in small slices or 'fingers' for your baby.

Makes 1 large quiche or 6 individual quiches

oil or butter (preferably unsalted) for frying

1 garlic clove, finely chopped or crushed

1 medium leek, finely chopped

175g (6oz) red lentils, rinsed in cold water
   and drained

600ml (1 pint) full-fat milk

pinch of dried thyme

250g (9oz) shortcrust pastry (see page 181), or 1 pre-baked
   pastry case (or, for individual pies, 300g/10½oz pastry)

2 eggs

75g (2½oz) cheese, grated

3 medium tomatoes, sliced

Heat the oil or butter in a pan, add the garlic and leek and fry until soft.

Add the lentils and stir. Add the milk and thyme and bring to the boil.

Reduce the heat, cover and simmer gently for 30–40 minutes, checking and stirring every 5 minutes until the lentils are soft and the mixture is nice and thick. Remove from the heat and set aside.

While the lentils are cooking, prepare your pastry case: either line a 23cm (9in) pie tin (or six 10cm/4in tins) with pastry (you can bake this 'blind' if you like – see pages 181–2) or use a ready-made pastry case.

Preheat the oven to 190°C/375°F/Gas Mark 5. In a bowl, beat the eggs and stir in half the cheese. Add the cheese and eggs to the lentil mixture and stir to mix.

Pour the mixture into the pastry case. Sprinkle with the remaining cheese and place the tomato slices on top.

Bake in the oven for about 45 minutes, until the egg is cooked through (test with a skewer) and the surface is golden brown.

Serve warm or cold, with new potatoes and vegetables, or a salad.

Frittata (Italian Omelette)

Frittata is a lovely recipe and the fillings can be varied so it's different every time. It can be made with freshly cooked vegetables but is also a great way to use up any leftovers.

Serves 2 adults and 1 baby

2 large potatoes (approx 400g/14oz)

4 eggs

1 tbsp milk

2 tsp chopped fresh parsley

pinch of freshly ground black pepper (optional)

oil for frying

1 medium onion, chopped

1–2 garlic cloves, chopped

filling of your choice (see options, below)

Steam or boil the potatoes until soft and allow to cool (or use previously boiled potatoes). Slice thinly and set aside.

Preheat the grill to Medium. Beat the eggs and milk together and stir in the parsley and black pepper.

Heat the oil in a 20cm (8in) frying pan with a flameproof handle. Add the onion and fry gently until soft. Add the garlic and cook for another minute or two, then add the potatoes and heat through, moving them around so that they don't stick.

Pour the egg mixture over the other ingredients in the frying pan. Stir once, quickly, to ensure they are all coated. Cook until the egg is thoroughly set (test by inserting a skewer – it should come out clean). Meanwhile, preheat the grill to Medium.

Put the pan under the grill for 3–5 minutes until the frittata begins to brown on top. Serve warm or cold, on its own or with vegetables or a salad.

Options

- The beauty of this recipe is that you can put almost any sautéed or pre-cooked vegetables or meat you want into it. Try chopped ham or bacon; pepper (green, red, yellow or orange) or aubergine; peas or green beans; mushrooms; broccoli or cauliflower; tomatoes; courgettes or butternut squash.
- Try sprinkling grated cheese on top of the frittata before you put it under the grill.

MAINS: VEGETABLE-BASED

There are plenty of textures and tastes for your baby to try out in our selection of healthy vegetable-based dishes.

Ratatouille

This dish is ideal for BLW beginners, as the vegetables can be cut into chunky sticks.

Serves 2 adults and 1 baby

oil for frying
1 large onion, sliced into thin rings
1 large aubergine, cut to suit your baby
1 pepper, preferably red, cut to suit your baby
2 courgettes, cut to suit your baby
2–3 garlic cloves, finely chopped or crushed
3–4 large ripe tomatoes (or a 400g/14oz tin of plum tomatoes)
1 tsp dried oregano
pinch of freshly ground black pepper
1 tbsp tomato purée (optional)

Heat the oil in a pan and fry the onion for a few minutes. Add the aubergine, pepper, courgettes and garlic and cook for 5–10 minutes, turning occasionally, until soft.

Meanwhile, blanch the tomatoes (if using fresh) in boiling water until the skins begin to split, then drain, immerse in cold water, remove the skins and roughly chop.

Add the oregano, black pepper and tomatoes to the pan, and stir well.

Continue to cook on a low heat for 20–30 minutes, until the tomatoes have made a thick sauce. Serve warm, with rice or pasta, as an accompaniment to a main dish such as quiche, or on its own with chunks of fresh bread and butter.

Tofu and Pepper Stir-Fry

Stir-fried tofu is usually marinated with soy sauce or tamari but, as these are too salty for babies, this recipe uses ginger and sesame oil, which give a lovely fresh flavour. Adults may like to add tamari or soy sauce to their own portion.

Serves 2 adults and 1 baby

150g (5½oz) firm tofu (not silken), cut into chunks to suit your baby

2–3cm (¾–1¼in) piece of fresh ginger, peeled and finely sliced

3 tbsp sesame oil

2 peppers (red, yellow or orange), thinly sliced lengthways

4 spring onions, roughly chopped

6–8 cherry or mini plum tomatoes

Put the tofu into a bowl with the ginger and 2 tbsp of the sesame oil, and leave it to marinate for 15 minutes.

Heat a large pan (preferably a wok) until very hot and add the rest of the sesame oil.

Add the ginger from the marinade and cook for 30 seconds or so. Add the peppers, spring onions and tomatoes and stir-fry for 5–10 minutes until tender, keeping the pan hot and stirring/tossing everything constantly.

Add the tofu (discarding the marinade) and stir-fry for about 2 minutes.

Serve warm with noodles, basmati or sticky rice. Halve the tomatoes in your baby's portion.

Option

• Adults may enjoy a handful of toasted sesame seeds, peanuts or cashew nuts added just before serving, together with a dash of soy sauce or tamari.

Mild Lentil and Vegetable Curry

This is a lovely gentle curry, which will introduce your baby to a range of flavours and textures – and there are plenty of shapes that he'll be able to get hold of easily if he's just starting out. If you can't find okras, you can use fine/dwarf green beans instead.

Serves 2 adults and 1 baby

- 1–2 tbsp oil
- 2 medium red onions, finely chopped
- 2 cardamom pods
- 1cm (½in) piece of fresh ginger, peeled and finely chopped
- approx 2 tbsp Quick Curry Paste (see pages 185–6)
- 1 bay leaf
- 2 new potatoes, skins on and halved or quartered, depending on size
- 3 broccoli florets, cut to suit your baby
- 3 cauliflower florets, cut to suit your baby
- 1 medium carrot, cut to suit your baby
- 3 okras, topped and tailed, and cut into pieces to suit your baby
- 2–3 tbsp frozen peas
- 1 small courgette, cut to suit your baby
- 100g (3½oz) red lentils, rinsed in cold water and drained
- 300ml (11fl oz) coconut milk

Heat the oil in a large pan, add the onions and fry gently for 10 minutes until they are golden. Meanwhile, split open the cardamom pods and remove the seeds (discard the pods). Add the seeds to the pan, with the ginger, curry paste and bay leaf, and fry for a few minutes, stirring occasionally to prevent everything from sticking.

Add the potatoes, broccoli, cauliflower, carrot and okra. Cook for a few minutes, stirring occasionally, to coat the vegetables in the spices.

Add the rest of the vegetables, together with the lentils and coconut milk.

Bring to the boil, cover, and simmer for 20 minutes until the lentils are tender and the vegetables are cooked, stirring occasionally to prevent food sticking and burning.

The liquid should now have reduced by half – simmer for a little longer with the lid off if you want a drier curry. Serve warm, with rice, natural yoghurt (or Yoghurt and Cucumber Dip, see page 74), salad and naan bread or chapattis (see page 167).

Saag Paneer

This gentle curry uses paneer, a mild white cheese which is especially useful when cooking for babies because it's unsalted. If you can't find paneer, the recipe works equally well with firm tofu (not 'silken').(Remember to wash your hands after handling the raw chilli, and before touching your baby because chilli juice can sting.)

Serves 2 adults and 1 baby

300g (10½oz) spinach

oil or butter (preferably unsalted) for frying

1 tsp cumin seeds

1 medium onion, sliced

2 garlic cloves, finely chopped or crushed

2–3cm (¾–1¼in) piece of fresh ginger, peeled and finely chopped

1 tbsp garam masala

¼ mild fresh chilli pepper (such as jalapeno), finely chopped (deseeded and veins removed), or a pinch of dried chilli flakes

225g (8oz) paneer cheese (or firm tofu), chopped to suit your baby

2 tbsp double cream

Lightly steam the spinach and blend it into a paste (an electric blender is best but a fork will do).

Heat the oil or butter in a large frying pan. Add the cumin seeds and fry for about 2 minutes until they start to become fragrant and make a popping sound. Add the onion and fry until soft. Add the garlic, ginger, garam masala and chilli, and stir. Add the spinach paste, with a little water, if required, to make a runny sauce. Bring to the boil, then reduce the heat.

Add the paneer (or tofu) and cream and simmer for about 3 minutes. Serve warm, with rice or naan bread.

Green Bean and Fennel Stir-Fry

This tasty stir-fry is light and fresh-tasting, and has plenty of stick shapes and strips to get hold of – slice them finely until your baby can deal with crunchier textures.

This recipe uses Japanese rice vinegar, which is much milder than Western vinegars. Many large supermarkets stock it, but if you can't find it, you can use wine vinegar diluted with water (three parts vinegar to one part water).

Serves 2 adults and 1 baby

25g (1oz) unsweetened desiccated coconut

warm water

100g (3½oz) noodles

1 tbsp oil for frying

1 garlic clove, finely chopped or crushed

4 spring onions, chopped

½ fennel bulb, core removed and sliced finely

100g (3½oz) fine/dwarf beans, whole or sliced in half
    lengthways (depending on how crunchy you want them)

100g (3½oz) mangetout, whole or sliced to suit your baby

1 medium celery stick, sliced into very thin sticks

2 tsp rice vinegar

1–2 tbsp chopped fresh coriander or parsley

Put the coconut into a bowl of warm water, cover, and leave for 20 minutes. Meanwhile, cook the noodles according to the instructions on the packet, then drain well and set aside. Strain the coconut through a sieve and set aside.

Heat a wok or large frying pan until very hot, add the oil and then the garlic, onions and fennel, and stir-fry for 2 minutes, keeping the pan very hot. Add the beans, mangetout and celery, and stir-fry briefly. Add the rice vinegar, stir, then remove the pan from the heat. Sprinkle on the coconut, coriander or parsley, and stir.

Arrange the noodles in serving bowls with the stir-fried vegetables on top. Serve warm, with, for adults, a dash of tamari or soy sauce.

Bean and Vegetable Chilli

'Grace really enjoys picking up the kidney beans in the vegetable chilli with her fingers. She'll eat them first and then pick out other bits.'

Kim, mother of Grace, 11 months

Serves 2 adults and 1 baby

oil for frying
1 medium onion, chopped
1 red pepper, deseeded and cut to suit your baby
1 medium courgette, cut to suit your baby
1 tsp ground cumin
pinch of chilli powder or flakes, or to taste
1 tsp dried coriander, or 1 tbsp chopped fresh coriander
400g (14oz) tin chopped tomatoes
400g (14oz) tin red kidney beans, drained (or approx 100g/3½oz
    dried beans, pre-cooked – see page 51)

Heat the oil in a pan and add the onion. Fry until soft. Add the pepper and courgette, and cook until they begin to soften. Add the spices and herbs and cook for 1 minute, stirring constantly.

Add the tomatoes and beans and mix well. Bring to the boil, cover and simmer for 15–20 minutes, until all the vegetables are soft.

Serve warm, with rice or couscous.

Options

• Any vegetables can be included in this chilli. Try swapping the pepper and courgette for some chopped mushrooms, squash, carrot or sweet potato (which may need to be cooked for a little longer). Chopped spinach can be added when the rest of the vegetables are soft, and cooked for just a few minutes.
• You can replace the red kidney beans with similar beans, such as cannellini or pinto. If using dried beans, they will need to be pre-soaked and possibly pre-cooked (see page 51).

MAINS: PIZZA, PASTA & RICE

Meals based on pizza, pasta or rice are usually a big hit with everyone in the family – and they generally contain a variety of shapes that babies will enjoy.

Home-made Pizza

Shop-bought and take-away pizzas are almost always high in salt, so making your own is a healthy option and means that you can confidently share the meal with your baby. Older children and toddlers usually love creating their own pizzas from scratch. Make your own base (or use shop-bought), add a thick tomato sauce, some cheese (traditionally mozzarella, although other cheeses, such as Cheddar, can be used) and your favourite toppings.

Makes 1 pizza, enough for 2 adults and 1 baby

For the dough:

3 tbsp olive oil, plus extra for greasing

225g (8oz) self-raising flour (or use plain flour with 2–3 tsp baking powder), plus extra for dusting

pinch of salt (optional)

90–100ml (3–3½fl oz) warm water

toppings of your choice (see overleaf)

For the sauce:

oil for frying

1 garlic clove, finely chopped or crushed

400ml (14fl oz) passata

2 tbsp tomato purée

1 tsp dried oregano

pinch of freshly ground black pepper

133

Lightly grease a pizza tray or large baking sheet. Put the flour into a bowl (with the salt, if using), and make a well in the centre. Pour in the oil and most of the water. Mix until you have an elastic (but not sticky) dough, adding more water as necessary.

Transfer the dough to a floured surface and knead until it is an even colour and feels uniformly elastic. Roll out the dough, shaping it into a round or oblong to fit your tray.

To make the sauce, heat the oil in a saucepan and fry the garlic for a minute or so. Add the remaining ingredients and simmer uncovered, so that the liquid reduces, for about 10 minutes, until the sauce is thick enough to cling to a pizza dough base.

Preheat the oven to 220°C/425°F/Gas Mark 7. Spread a generous layer of thick tomato sauce over the pizza base. Sprinkle with grated cheese and add any additional toppings, including a final layer of cheese, if you like.

Put the pizza in the oven and bake for 10–20 minutes, until the top is bubbling in the middle.

Suggested toppings

Almost anything can be used as a pizza topping, but here are some favourites:

- Chopped bacon, ham or salami (not too much – these are very salty)
- Lean minced beef or shredded chicken
- Sardines (in oil, not brine)
- Sliced tomatoes, or halved cherry tomatoes
- Sliced mushrooms
- Sweetcorn
- Sliced red, yellow or green peppers
- Spinach, broccoli or leek
- Mozzarella cheese
- Olives (in olive oil, not brine)

Pasta

Pasta is the perfect quick and easy meal for busy families. Many sauces can easily be prepared beforehand and are ideal for batch cooking and freezing; if you are really in a hurry, simply serve it with a spoonful of pesto (see page 184–5 for a home-made version). Choose pasta shapes to suit your baby's dexterity.

Cooking pasta

Pasta needs to move while cooking to stop it sticking together, so it's best to cook it in a large pan with plenty of water, which is kept boiling vigorously. Although many traditionalists say it should be cooked in salted water, as long as you're careful not to overcook the pasta, the texture should be fine when cooked without salt, which is better for babies. Don't add oil while it's cooking – it will prevent any sauce coating the pasta properly later, and make it more slippery for your baby to hold. For best results, follow the instructions on the packet for the recommended cooking time – but take a piece out to test for texture a minute or so before the recommended time is up.

Simple Tomato Pasta Sauce

This simple sauce is ideal for serving with pasta and is easy to make in batches for freezing. It's delicious mixed with grilled or roasted courgette, aubergine and peppers, or as the basis for other sauces, such as Bolognese (see page 138). It can also be served with chicken and fish.

Makes about 300ml (11fl oz)

2 tbsp olive oil
1 medium onion, finely chopped
1–2 garlic cloves, finely chopped or crushed
400g (14 oz) tin chopped tomatoes (or 400ml/14fl oz passata)
2 tbsp tomato purée
a handful of fresh basil leaves, torn
pinch of freshly ground black pepper
1 bay leaf

Heat the oil in a pan, add the onion and fry gently until soft. Add the garlic and cook gently for another minute or two, then add the tomatoes. Stir in the tomato purée, basil and black pepper, then add the bay leaf. Simmer gently for about 20 minutes. Remove the bay leaf, blend the sauce if you wish, then serve warm with pasta.

Options

- Try spicing this sauce up by adding a few dried chilli flakes.
- Add some some finely grated celery and carrot with the onion for extra flavour.
- Try using fresh plum or cherry tomatoes (chopped or halved) with some passata, instead of tinned tomatoes.

Tuna and Tomato Pasta

This is a really simple, tasty, store-cupboard pasta dish that can be prepared in no time.

Serves 2 adults and 1 baby

225g (8oz) pasta shapes
oil for frying
1 medium red onion, finely chopped
185g (6½oz) tin tuna steaks (in spring water or oil, not brine)
1 garlic clove, finely chopped or crushed
1 tsp dried mixed herbs/herbes de Provence
400g (14oz) tin chopped tomatoes, or 400ml (14fl oz) passata
   (or half-and-half)
dash of balsamic vinegar, to taste

Cook the pasta in a pan of boiling water according to the instructions on the packet, then drain well.

Meanwhile, make the sauce. Heat the oil in a pan and fry the onion for a few minutes, until soft. Break up the tuna and add it to the pan along with the garlic. Cook for 2–3 minutes. Add the herbs and stir to mix. Add the tomatoes or passata and the balsamic vinegar, and stir. Allow to simmer for about 5 minutes, or longer if you want a thicker sauce.

Pour the sauce over the pasta and serve with a side salad.

Macaroni Cheese

This tasty favourite tends to be a bit salty, so don't offer it to your baby too often. You can add some vegetables to the sauce to make it a more balanced meal. For an alternative way to make the sauce, see page 188.

'Callum really enjoys macaroni cheese. We always put broccoli, onions and cauliflower in it. He carefully picks out the onions and then eats the rest.'
Helen, mother of Callum, 11 months

Serves 2 adults and 1 baby

225g (8oz) macaroni (or other tubular or spiral pasta shapes)
25g (1oz) butter (preferably unsalted)
25g (1oz) plain flour
300ml (11fl oz) milk
50–100g (2oz–3½oz) cheese, grated (a mix of Parmesan and Cheddar is good)
a splash of Worcestershire sauce, to taste (optional)
nutmeg, for grating, or ½ tsp ready-ground nutmeg (optional)
40g (1½oz) breadcrumbs (optional)
8–10 cherry tomatoes, halved (optional)

Preheat the oven to 200°C/400°F/Gas Mark 6. Cook the pasta in a pan of boiling water according to the instructions on the packet, then drain well.

Meanwhile, make the sauce. Melt the butter in a pan and stir in the flour. Cook gently for 2–3 minutes until the mixture starts to bubble. Remove the pan from the heat and gradually add the milk, stirring constantly. Return the pan to the heat and bring to the boil, still stirring. Simmer until thickened, stirring all the time. Remove from the heat and stir in almost all of the cheese, with the Worcestershire sauce and a little nutmeg. Tip in the cooked pasta and stir well.

Pour the mixture into an ovenproof dish, then sprinkle with the remaining cheese and the breadcrumbs and arrange the cherry tomatoes on top (cut-side up). Put into the oven and bake for 10–20 minutes, until the cheese is bubbly and beginning to turn brown.

Serve warm, with salad or vegetables.

Bolognese Sauce

Most babies love Bolognese sauce, and as soon as they can they will pick up handfuls and push it into their mouths. If you leave some of the meat in clumps while you are frying it, your baby will find it easier to pick up. And if you plan to serve the sauce with spaghetti, have your camera ready – it can be fantastically messy! Many people say Bolognese sauce tastes better made several hours before you plan to eat it, then kept in the fridge so the flavours can mature (be sure to reheat it thoroughly before serving). If you are making the sauce for a lasagne (see page 140), add a little water during the cooking if necessary, to keep it runny.

Serves 2 adults and 1 baby

20g (¾oz) bacon lardons or 1 rasher of streaky bacon, finely chopped (using scissors is easiest)

1 medium red onion, finely chopped

oil for frying (if needed)

200g (7oz) lean minced beef

1 garlic clove, finely chopped or crushed (optional)

1 medium carrot, finely chopped or grated

1 celery stick, strings removed and finely chopped

50g (2oz) mushrooms, sliced

400g tin (14oz) tomatoes, chopped

1 tbsp tomato purée

1–2 tsp dried oregano or 1 tbsp fresh oregano leaves

1 bay leaf

small bunch of fresh basil leaves, torn

freshly ground black pepper, to taste (optional)

approx 40g (1½oz) Parmesan cheese, to serve

Heat a large pan and add the bacon and onion. Fry until the onion is soft (the bacon will be fatty so you probably won't need any oil). Add the minced beef and cook for about 5 minutes until the mince is browned. Add the garlic and cook for another minute. Add the carrot, celery, mushrooms, tomatoes, tomato purée and oregano, and mix well. Add the bay leaf, bring to the boil, cover and simmer for 20 minutes. Check occasionally, and add a little water if the sauce appears too thick.

Just before serving, remove the bay leaf and add the torn basil leaves, along with some black pepper, if desired. Top with freshly grated or shaved Parmesan cheese.

Serve warm, with a pasta of your choice – either mixed in or poured over the top – on its own or with a green salad.

Options

- You can make a similar sauce with minced pork, or a mixture of pork and beef.
- If you have some ready-made Simple Tomato Sauce (see page 135–6), just fry the mince, stir in the sauce and cook until it's thoroughly heated through.

Pasta with Asparagus

'We offered Tom asparagus and I think he thought it was a green bean – which he loves – but he looked really puzzled and disappointed. I don't think it was that he didn't like the asparagus – just that it wasn't what he was expecting.'

Liz, mother of Tom, 2 years

Serves 2 adults and 1 baby

225g (8oz) pasta shapes

12 medium-sized whole asparagus spears

approx 25g (1oz) butter (preferably unsalted)

2 garlic cloves, crushed

1 tbsp chopped fresh basil

25g (1oz) Parmesan cheese, grated

Cook the pasta in a pan of boiling water according to the instructions on the packet, then drain well. Meanwhile trim the asparagus spears by chopping off any woody bits at the base of the stem. Steam the trimmed tips for 5 minutes, or until tender.

Melt the butter gently in a large pan. Add the garlic and cook gently for 30 seconds. Stir in the drained pasta and basil. Mix in the asparagus spears so they are coated in butter.

Sprinkle with Parmesan cheese and serve warm, with a green salad.

Options

- Green beans, sliced runner beans or broccoli can be used instead of asparagus.
- You can add a 185g (6½oz) tin tuna (in oil, not brine) when you stir in the pasta.
- Try fresh parsley or sage in place of the basil.

139

Classic Lasagne

Many babies enjoy dismantling the layers of a lasagne and eating the different bits individually, but beginners may find it tricky to pick up, so it's a good idea to serve it alongside something easy to manage, such as broccoli.

The two main sauces in a lasagne (usually Bolognese and a béchamel or cheese sauce) lend themselves to batch cooking, so if you already have some made, this dish is fairly quick to prepare – especially if you buy lasagne sheets that don't need pre-boiling. If you are starting from scratch you will need to allow plenty of time. The size of your dish will determine how many layers deep your lasagne is. Choose a wide dish if you only want a couple of layers.

Make sure your sauces are fairly runny because the lasagne sheets will absorb water from them. Just add a little water (to Bolognese sauce) or milk (to béchamel or cheese sauce) as necessary.

Serves 2 adults and 1 baby, very generously

1 batch of Bolognese sauce (page 138)

quick-cook lasagne sheets (up to 10 sheets)

2–3 batches of béchamel or cheese sauce (see pages 187–8)

3 medium tomatoes, sliced (optional)

**approx 50g (2oz) Parmesan cheese, grated (optional – you may
    need less if you are using a cheese sauce)**

grated nutmeg

Preheat the oven to 190°C/375°F/Gas Mark 5. Put a shallow layer of Bolognese sauce in the bottom of an ovenproof dish. Cover with a single layer of lasagne sheets, breaking them as necessary to minimise overlapping. Pour over a layer of béchamel/cheese sauce. Repeat these three layers up to three more times, depending on the width of your dish, making sure the last layer is béchamel/cheese sauce.

Arrange the tomato slices on top and sprinkle with Parmesan cheese and nutmeg. Put into the oven and bake for about 30 minutes, until browned on top.

Serve warm, cut into rough slices, with a simple green salad or some broccoli or green beans.

Portobello Mushroom Carbonara

Carbonara sauce is traditionally made with raw eggs, but this delicious version gets by without them. Slices of large Portobello mushrooms will give your baby an easy shape to handle, but smaller mushrooms will taste just as good.

Serves 2 adults and 1 baby

225g (8oz) pasta shapes

50g (2oz) butter (preferably unsalted)

2 rashers lean bacon, cut into small pieces

4 large Portobello mushrooms, cut into thick slices

1–2 garlic cloves, finely chopped or crushed

250ml (9fl oz) single cream

1 tbsp chopped fresh parsley or basil

25g (1oz) Parmesan cheese, grated

Cook the pasta in a pan of boiling water according to the instructions on the packet, then drain well.

Melt the butter gently in a large pan. Add the pieces of bacon and cook over a low heat for 1 minute. Add the sliced mushrooms and garlic and cook for another 2 minutes. Stir in the single cream and parsley or basil, and continue cooking gently for a further 3–4 minutes, stirring occasionally.

Pour the sauce over the pasta and sprinkle with Parmesan cheese.

Serve warm, with a green salad.

Rice

Rice is great for helping babies to develop their self-feeding skills, but there's no need to aim for 'perfect' light, fluffy rice when your baby is just starting out; most babies do better with rice that they can pick up in clumps, such as Thai sticky rice, Japanese sushi rice or risotto rice. If long grain rice is all you have in the house, just overcook it slightly, so that it sticks together. Later, once your baby starts using a pincer grip, he'll enjoy picking up individual grains.

Rice should be washed in cold water before cooking. (The exception is rice produced in the USA, which is fortified with a coating of vitamins which would be lost if it were rinsed.)

As a general rule, rice needs to absorb roughly its own volume of water (that is, a cup of rice will absorb a cup of water), although more needs to be added to allow for water lost as steam. However, cooking rice in too much water makes it sticky – as does boiling it too rapidly and stirring it while it's cooking. Basmati rice is traditionally pre-soaked to keep the grains separate when cooked (it's then fluffed up with a fork before serving). In general, when cooking rice, follow the packet instructions for the best results.

> '*It helps if the rice is a bit stickier and not broken up too much. We have basmati and I just serve Safia hers before I stir the rest to fluff it up.*'
>
> Farida, mother of Azraa, 2 years, and Safia, 8 months

Risotto

Risotto is a great dish for baby-led weaning. It's one of the easiest ways for babies to eat rice in the early weeks – they pick up soft handfuls of the delicious, creamy rice and push or squeeze it into their mouth. There are many ingredients you can add to a risotto, and the sizes and shapes can be easily adapted to suit your baby. Risotto also sticks well to spoons, allowing your older baby to practise using cutlery.

You'll get the best texture using a proper risotto rice, preferably arborio or carnaroli. Add Parmesan cheese and a little butter at the end to help it stick together.

When you are making risotto, the stock should remain hot while you are adding it, so keep it simmering in a pan next to the risotto and add a small ladleful at a time. A traditional risotto needs almost constant stirring, which may be fine when your baby is snuggled up in a sling, or fast asleep, but not so easy if he needs your attention, so we've included an oven-baked alternative. Leftovers (if you have any) can be used to make Arancini (see page 70).

Colourful Chicken Risotto

This risotto gives your baby lots of different shapes, flavours and colours to explore.

Serves 2 adults and 1 baby

1 tbsp olive oil

25–50g (1–2oz) butter (preferably unsalted)

1 small onion, chopped or sliced

200–300g (7–10½oz) chicken, cut to suit your baby

**approx 750ml (26fl oz) chicken stock (low-salt or home-made –
  see pages 182–3)**

1 small red pepper, deseeded and cut to suit your baby

1 small courgette, cut to suit your baby

1 handful sweetcorn (tinned or frozen) (optional)

250g (9oz) (about ¾ of a mugful) risotto rice

2 tbsp grated Parmesan cheese

freshly ground black pepper, to taste

Heat the oil and butter in a large pan. When the butter is melted, add the onion and fry until soft. Add the chicken and fry gently until the outside is sealed and white.

Meanwhile, put the stock on to heat in a separate pan.

Add the pepper and courgette to the chicken, and fry gently for a further 3–4 minutes, until they start to soften, then add the sweetcorn (if using). Add the rice and stir to make sure that all the grains have a light coating of the butter/oil mixture (add a little more butter or oil if necessary).

Add the hot stock to the rice mixture, a ladleful at a time, stirring constantly, until each ladleful is absorbed. Simmer gently. Continue adding stock (you may not need all of it) until the rice is plump but still has a 'bite', and the overall consistency in the pan is creamy (this will take about 20–25 minutes).

Take the pan off the heat, stir in the Parmesan cheese and black pepper, and serve.

Options

- You can use different vegetables, such as peas or mushrooms.
- This dish is also delicious made without the chicken and using vegetable stock instead of the chicken stock.

Mushroom Risotto

This risotto can be made with any type of mushroom, but using large mushrooms (such as Portobello) will give your baby a better chance of picking the pieces up individually, if he's just starting out.

Serves 2 adults and 1 baby

approx 750ml (26fl oz) chicken stock (low-salt or home-made –
  see pages 182–3)
2 tbsp olive oil
1 small onion, finely chopped
1 garlic clove, finely chopped or crushed (optional)
200g (7oz) fresh mushrooms, sliced (chestnut or Portobello
  are good)
250g (9oz) (about ¾ of a mugful) risotto rice
knob of butter (preferably unsalted)
25g (1oz) Parmesan cheese, grated
freshly ground black pepper, to taste
2 tbsp chopped fresh parsley (optional)

Put the stock on to heat in a pan.

Heat the oil in a second, large pan, add the onion and fry until soft. Add the garlic, and after a few seconds add the mushrooms. Fry for a couple of minutes. Add the rice and stir to make sure that all the grains have a light coating of oil.

Add the hot stock, a ladleful at a time, stirring constantly, until each ladleful is absorbed. Simmer gently. Continue adding stock (you may not need all of it) until the rice is plump but still has a 'bite', and the overall consistency in the pan is creamy (this will take 20–25 minutes).

Take the pan off the heat and add the butter, Parmesan cheese and black pepper. Stir well and serve, sprinkled with chopped parsley.

Option

• A few grilled fresh mushrooms make a good topping.

Oven-baked Aubergine and Courgette Risotto

This risotto is an easier option if you don't have the time to stand and stir a dish on the hob and, as with all risottos, your baby will love picking up the soft handfuls of rice. If he still needs stick shapes, the aubergine and courgette can easily be cut up to suit him.

Serves 2 adults and 1 baby, generously

500–600ml (18–21fl oz) vegetable stock (low-salt or home-made – see page 183)

2 tbsp olive oil

1 medium onion, chopped

2 garlic cloves, finely chopped or crushed

1 small aubergine, cut to suit your baby

1 medium courgette, cut to suit your baby

250g (9oz) (about ¾ of a mugful) risotto rice

knob of butter (optional)

60g (2oz) Parmesan cheese, grated

freshly ground black pepper, to taste (optional)

Preheat the oven to 200°C/400°F/Gas Mark 6 and put the stock on to heat in a pan.

Heat the oil (preferably in a flameproof casserole, so you don't have to transfer the food at the next stage). Add the onion and fry until soft.

Add the garlic, and after a few seconds add the other vegetables. Cook until they start to soften.

Add the rice and stir to make sure that all the grains have a light coating of oil. Add 500ml (18fl oz) stock and bring to the boil.

Cover the dish (or transfer the mixture from the pan to an ovenproof casserole) and put it in the oven to cook for 30 minutes, then stir gently and add more hot stock if necessary. Bake for another 10 minutes.

Remove from the oven, check the texture of the rice; if cooked, add the butter (if using), Parmesan cheese and black pepper, and stir again.

Cover the dish and leave it to rest for a few minutes before serving.

Mild Vegetable Biryani

This dish is a tasty accompaniment to curries, making a change from plain rice.
The rice is soaked before cooking to help the grains stay separate – perfect for when
your baby is able to pick up tiny things!

*'Sean was so happy when he got the hang of his pincer grip and he could pick up
peas. He just loved it – he'd spend ages picking them up really carefully one at a
time, and he'd eat loads. He'd be there for ages.'*

Pam, mother of Sean, 13 months

Serves 2 adults and 1 baby

100g (3½oz) basmati rice

1 tbsp sunflower oil

1 tsp cumin seeds

1 large carrot, finely chopped

150g (5½oz) frozen peas

1 garlic clove, finely chopped or crushed

pinch of chilli powder

boiling water

> **Tip:** *Mix some thick
> natural yoghurt in with
> the finished dish to make it
> easier for babies to pick up
> in handfuls.*

Wash the rice and soak it in a bowl of cold water for about 30 minutes before cooking.
Warm the oil and cumin seeds in a pan (don't allow the seeds to get
too brown). Add the drained rice, vegetables, garlic
and chilli powder, and stir to mix. Pour on boiling
water to cover the ingredients by about 1cm
(½in). Cover with a lid, bring back to the boil
and simmer for 10–15 minutes, until the water
has been absorbed and the rice is plump.
Fluff up with a fork and serve with a
curry.

SIDES & VEGETABLES

Babies starting out with solids often have more fun with the sides than the main dish, so it's good to keep them varied to give your baby plenty of new things to try.

Preparing and Cooking Vegetables

All vegetables should be washed in cold water thoroughly before cooking, especially leeks and leafy vegetables, such as loose heads of cabbage, which sometimes have mud between the leaves. If they are not organic it's best to peel root vegetables thinly, as fertilisers and pesticides tend to accumulate in the skin.

Steamed and Boiled Vegetables

Cut your vegetables into pieces of the right shape and size for your baby (see page 25). Try to make sure that vegetables of the same type are cut into pieces that are roughly the same size so that they cook in the same amount of time:

- **Root vegetables**, such as carrots and parsnips: cut into thick shapes
- **Potatoes**: cut into halves, quarters or smaller, depending on size. Small new potatoes can be cooked whole
- **Leafy vegetables**: shred, tear or leave whole
- **Broccoli and cauliflower**: cut into florets with some stalk left on
- **Green beans**: trim the ends (topping and tailing) and remove any stringy bits; dwarf beans (also called fine or French beans) can be left whole or snapped in half but runner beans need to be sliced
- **Brussels sprouts**: trim any ragged leaves and cut a 'X' in the bottom of each one (to help them to cook quickly)

147

Steamed vegetables

Steaming vegetables retains more flavour, texture, nutrients and colour than boiling. If you don't have a steamer, you can use an ordinary saucepan with a small metal steamer basket or an upturned saucer in the bottom. Vegetables can also be 'steamed' in a microwave.

On the hob: bring some water to the boil in a steamer and cover with a lid for a minute or two. Check that the water is not bubbling into the steamer basket – if it is, empty some water out. Put the vegetables that will take the longest to cook into the steamer first (potatoes and carrots, for example) and put the lid on. Part of the way through cooking, add the faster-cooking vegetables (preferably in a separate section – if not, just add to the other vegetables, taking care not to overload, as the steam needs to circulate freely).

The cooking time depends on the type of vegetable, how much is in the pan, how small you cut the pieces, and how crunchy you want them. In general, though, hard root vegetables (such as potatoes) take longest; loose green leaves (such as cabbage) cook more quickly. Test with a knife, or by tasting, to check that the vegetables are firm enough for your baby to hold but soft enough for her to munch.

In a microwave: place the prepared vegetables in a microwave-proof bowl with a little water in the bottom. Cover with a loose lid or cling film (pierce a few holes with a skewer or sharp knife). Cooking time will depend on the type of vegetable and how tender you want it to be. Root vegetables, such as potatoes and carrots, take longer to cook, and need to be cooked separately from leafy vegetables.

Approximate cooking times for steaming on the hob

Spinach/pak choi:	1–2 minutes
Leafy greens:	3–5 minutes (they'll turn bright green when cooked)
Broccoli/cauliflower:	5–10 minutes (test for tenderness)
Green beans:	10 minutes (test for tenderness)
Asparagus:	10 minutes (test for tenderness)
Carrots:	15 minutes (test for tenderness)
Brussels sprouts:	15 minutes (test for tenderness)
Sweetcorn (on the cob):	15 minutes (test for tenderness)
Yams:	20–25 minutes (test for tenderness)
Potatoes:	20–30 minutes (test for softness)

Boiled vegetables

Although most vegetables are more nutritious steamed, boiling is quicker, and some vegetables, such as frozen peas, tend to taste better boiled. Putting potatoes into cold water, and then bringing it to the boil encourages them to retain less starch; other vegetables (and new potatoes) are best cooked in already boiling water, so that the cooking time is as short as possible and the maximum amount of vitamins is retained.

When the vegetables have been added to the pan, the water should be brought back to the boil, then the pan covered and the vegetables allowed to simmer until they are tender. Cooking times will be slightly less than for steaming; test with a sharp knife when you think they are done. If preferred, vegetables can be cooked in stock (low salt or home-made, see page 183) rather than plain water, for extra flavour.

Roasted Vegetables

Roasting vegetables gives them a lovely sweet taste and makes them easy for babies to grip. It is also a very practical option if you already have the oven on for another dish; most vegetables will roast successfully in an oven set to above or below 200°C/400°F/Gas Mark 6, depending on what else you are cooking at the time. Remember, though, that the hotter the temperature, the smaller the pieces need to be – so that the outside doesn't burn before the inside is cooked. The same basic method applies to all types of vegetables, though the cooking time varies. If you need to speed things up some harder vegetables, such as potatoes, can be parboiled for 5–10 minutes before roasting.

Roast potatoes

Preheat the oven to 200°C/400°F/Gas Mark 6. Prepare the potatoes by peeling (or scrubbing) them, then chop into even-sized pieces. Put into a large pan of cold water and bring to the boil. Boil for about 5–10 minutes, then drain well using a colander. (Parboiling before roasting makes potatoes nice and crunchy on the outside.)

Give the potatoes a shake in the colander – the more you shake them, the crispier they'll be. Don't overdo it, though, or your baby may not be able to manage them.

Dry the potatoes, then heat enough oil in a small roasting tin to just cover the bottom (on the hob is fine). Add the potatoes and baste, turn or shake to make sure all surfaces have a thin coating of oil. Check there is a little space around each potato, then roast for about 1 hour (less for small pieces), turning again halfway through.

Potato wedges and chips

Wedges and chips are easier for small hands to hold and cook more quickly than ordinary roast potatoes. Both sweet potatoes and ordinary potatoes are delicious cooked this way.

Preheat the oven to 200°C/400°F/Gas Mark 6. Leave the skins on and cut the potatoes into wedge-shaped segments (or thick chip shapes), putting them into a bowl of cold water as you go. Drain and dry in a clean tea towel.

Heat enough oil in a small roasting tin to just cover the bottom (on the hob is fine), then add the wedges and baste, turn or shake them to make sure all surfaces have a thin coating of oil. Check there is a little space around each wedge, then roast them in the oven for about 30–40 minutes.

Roasted winter vegetables

A good mix of winter vegetables is carrots, parsnips, beetroot, onion and squash (or pumpkin).

Preheat the oven to 200°C/400°F/Gas Mark 6. Peel, then halve the carrots and parsnips (quarter them if they are very big, but don't cut them too small because they tend to shrink quite a bit when roasted). Cut any hard core out of the middle.

Peel the beetroot and onion and cut into chunks.

Leave the skin on the squash (so the pieces keep their shape and your baby can hold them easily) and cut into wedges or chunks.

Heat enough oil in a small roasting tin to just cover the bottom (on the hob is fine), then add the vegetables and baste, turn or shake them to make sure all surfaces have a thin coating of oil. Check there is a little space around each piece, then roast for 30–40 minutes.

Roasted summer vegetables

Aubergine, courgettes, red, orange or yellow peppers, tomato, fennel, red onions and garlic make a tasty roasted vegetable selection. They can be made into a main dish, by stirring them into couscous or pasta, or eaten cold as a salad.

Preheat the oven to 200°C/400°F/Gas Mark 6. Leave the skin on the vegetables (except the onion) and cut into pieces of roughly the same size. Courgettes can be halved lengthways, peppers quartered (with the seeds removed), and aubergine, onion and fennel cut into big chunks. Bulbs of garlic and tomatoes can be roasted whole.

Tip: *Potatoes can be roasted with other vegetables, but they need to be cut into smaller chunks or wedges to cook in the same time (potatoes should be about half the size of the other vegetables).*

Heat enough oil in a small roasting tin to just cover the bottom (on the hob is fine), then add the vegetables and baste, turn or shake them to make sure all surfaces have a thin coating of oil. Check there is a little space around each piece, then roast until tender for 20–30 minutes.

> **Tip:** *Try adding herbs, such as rosemary or thyme, to the vegetables before roasting – or for a tangy flavour, marinate them for an hour or so in a mixture of olive oil and balsamic vinegar.*

Grilled vegetables

Vegetables such as peppers, aubergines, courgettes and tomatoes are delicious grilled, and are perfect for babies who are just starting BLW.

'Riley hated steamed courgettes, but he loved them grilled – they were so much nicer, they were his favourites for ages.'

Cath, mother of Riley, 2 years

Preheat the grill to High. Halve any tomatoes and chop other vegetables into thick strips. Brush them with a little oil and put them under the hot grill.

Turn the vegetables (except the tomatoes) over after about 10 minutes, so that both sides are cooked. Most vegetables will take around 20 minutes to grill, depending on thickness. Check for tenderness when you think they are done.

Mashed potatoes and other vegetables

Many root vegetables can be mashed, so there's no need to stick to the classic mashed potato. Sweet potatoes, yams, carrot, turnip and swede are also good, either on their own, mixed with mashed potato (to give some colour and a sweeter taste to the potato), or in combinations – carrot with swede, for example.

Steam or boil the vegetables for about 20–25 minutes, making sure they are cooked until soft, then drain as necessary.

Mash with a masher, large fork or hand-held blender, adding a little butter (preferably unsalted) and milk (or cream) as you mash to make it less dry. Add a little ground black pepper to taste. Serve immediately.

Options

- Try adding grated cheese or a finely chopped spring onion to mashed potato.
- For extra creamy mashed potatoes, boil the potatoes in milk instead of water. Use just enough milk to come almost halfway up the potatoes. When they are cooked, mash them with the milk and add a knob of butter.

151

Couscous

Couscous is very quick and easy to cook and makes a nice change from rice or pasta. Most couscous sold in supermarkets is the 'instant' type, which cooks very quickly, just by adding boiling water. (Plain couscous is better than the flavoured varieties, as these often have salt added to them.) Authentic couscous needs to be steamed and takes longer. Just follow the instructions on the packet of whichever type you buy.

Options

- Try mixing some finely chopped onion or garlic into the dry couscous before adding the water, or stir in some chopped fresh herbs just before serving.
- Add some vegetables, such as strips of roasted peppers or steamed beetroot (chopped or sliced as necessary), to cooked couscous to make a colourful and tasty side dish.

> **Tip:** *To give rice or couscous more flavour, cook it in low-salt or home-made meat or vegetable stock rather than water.*

Dumplings

Dumplings are an old-fashioned recipe but they are a great way to help your little one to manage soup or stew with her fingers, and they are usually cooked in the same pan.

Makes about 8 dumplings

50g (2oz) self-raising flour, plus extra for dusting

25g (1oz) suet (shredded) or very cold butter, grated

1 tsp dried mixed herbs (optional)

pinch of freshly ground black pepper (optional)

Mix together the flour, suet or butter, herbs and black pepper (if using). Add just enough cold water to hold everything together and mix well to form an elastic dough.

Divide the mixture into about 16 pieces and roll each piece into a ball. Add the balls to the simmering soup or stew for the last 20 minutes of cooking time.

Option

- For extra flavour, add half a small onion (finely grated) and 1 tsp chopped fresh thyme, 1 tbsp chopped fresh parsley or 1 tsp caraway seeds.

Home-made Tomato Ketchup

If you like ketchup but don't want to introduce your baby to it because of the large amount of sugar and additives that it usually contains, try this home-made version instead. It will keep for a few days in the fridge or you can freeze it in small quantities.

Makes about 220ml (7½fl oz)

200ml (7fl oz) passata
2 tsp tomato purée
1 tbsp cider vinegar
1 garlic clove, finely chopped or crushed
¼ onion, finely chopped
¼ stick of celery, finely chopped
2 cloves
1 bay leaf
pinch of allspice
pinch of paprika

Combine all the ingredients in a saucepan and mix well. Bring to the boil and simmer for 5 minutes, stirring occasionally. Remove from the heat and allow to cool.

Remove the cloves and bay leaf, and blend the ketchup (with an electric blender) before serving.

Option

• Try adding some chilli powder for a spicier ketchup.

153

Spicy Tomato Salsa

Spicy tomato salsa goes well with home-made burgers, grilled fish and chicken.
It can also be used to spice up sandwiches and wraps, and is great for babies once
they can get soft handfuls of food to their mouth. This salsa is best eaten very fresh.
(Remember to wash your hands after handling raw chilli, and before touching your
baby because chilli juice can sting.)

Makes about 250g (9oz)

2–3 large ripe tomatoes (or the equivalent in cherry tomatoes)
1 garlic clove
2 spring onions (or 1 small red onion)
approx 1 tsp fresh chilli (deseeded and veins removed)
  or chilli flakes (according to taste)
juice of ½ lemon (approx 2 tsp) or ½ lime (approx 2 tsp)
1 tbsp olive oil
1–2 tbsp chopped fresh parsley or coriander

Chop the tomatoes, garlic, onions and fresh chilli as finely as you can (or use a food
processor – but don't let the ingredients turn to mush).

Mix the lemon (or lime) juice and the olive oil in a large bowl. Add the tomato
mixture and the parsley or coriander, and mix well.

Chill for a few minutes before serving.

Option

• Any of the following can be added to a basic spicy tomato salsa: chopped basil;
finely chopped cucumber; finely chopped red pepper; finely chopped avocado;
chopped mint leaves.

DESSERTS

Sweet desserts aren't really essential, but they can be a nutritious part of your family's diet – provided they don't contain large amounts of sugar or artificial sweeteners. Some of the recipes that follow include a little sugar, but they have plenty of other healthy ingredients and are far less sugary than shop-bought desserts. Many traditional recipes can be adapted by reducing the amount of sugar or replacing it with fresh or dried fruit. Adding spices, such as cinnamon, can also enhance sweetness.

Although recipes that use cooking apples usually include sugar, you may find that your baby enjoys the natural tartness of the fruit. Alternatively, you can use naturally sweet dessert apples in most recipes, but take care to choose fruit with plenty of flavour.

Of course, the simplest dessert is probably raw fresh fruit, either on its own or with full-fat natural yoghurt (preferably live), for dipping or having a go with a spoon. A range of fruit can give your baby great practice at handling different textures.

Simple Dessert Ideas

Fruit salad

A fruit salad is best made with fresh, seasonal fruits, but you can add thawed frozen fruit or tinned fruit (in its own juice, not in syrup). Wash, peel and cut the fruit (add bananas at the last minute as they go brown quickly when peeled). A little fruit juice can also be added. Serve as soon as possible. If you need to make the salad in advance, add a dash of lemon juice, cover and put it in the fridge.

'Liam loves oranges. He'll suck the juice out of a segment, then throw it away, get another segment and keep going until he's had enough.'

Frances, mother of Noah, 2 years, and Liam, 12 months

Natural fruit jelly

It's great fun to watch a baby handling jelly! For a sugar-free version all you need is about 20g (¾oz) powdered or leaf gelatine (vegetarian gelatine is available from health food shops) and 500ml (17½fl oz) pure fruit juice. Prepare the gelatine according to the instructions on the packet. Warm the fruit juice in a pan, add the gelatine and stir until fully dissolved. Pour the mixture into a dish, allow it to cool, then leave it to set in the fridge for a few hours. If you like, you can add pieces of chopped fruit, such as satsuma or pineapple, just before putting the jelly into the fridge.

Iced bananas

These are a great alternative to ice cream. Just peel and mash some ripe bananas and press the mixture into ice lolly moulds or a freezerproof container, then freeze for 3–4 hours, until firm. Remove from the freezer and allow to stand for at least 10 minutes at room temperature before serving.

Fruit and yoghurt lollies

These make a lovely summer dessert. Just blend about 300g (10½oz) of any fresh, frozen or tinned fruit (in its own juice, not syrup) with 500g (1lb 2oz) full-fat thick (Greek-style) natural yoghurt (preferably live). Pour the mixture into ice lolly moulds and freeze until set. Allow them to stand for 10 minutes at room temperature before eating. If you want a softer lolly, add around 1 tbsp of double cream to the mixture. Eat within a day or so of making.

Baked Apple Bombs

This is a deliciously sweet dessert, and full of goodness. Babies starting out will probably be able to get hold of large pieces of apple, cut into wedges; leave the skin on to make them easier to grip.

Serves 2 adults and 1 baby

about 150ml (5fl oz) apple juice (or a knob of butter, preferably unsalted)
3 dessert or cooking apples
4–6 dates, stones removed
60g (2oz) sultanas or raisins (optional)
pinch of ground cinnamon or nutmeg (optional)

Preheat the oven to 190°C/375°F/Gas Mark 5. Pour most of the apple juice into the bottom of an ovenproof dish (or use the butter to grease the dish).

Core the apples (keeping them whole and unpeeled) and place them in the dish.

Fill the centres of the apples with the dates and sultanas or raisins, and pour the rest of the apple juice over the top.

Sprinkle with cinnamon or nutmeg (if using) and put into the oven. Bake for about 40 minutes, or until the apples are soft.

Serve warm with natural yoghurt, crème fraîche or home-made custard (see page 161).

Options

- You can use pears instead of apples (choose squat round ones rather than long thin ones). Both apples and pears are delicious stuffed with a combination of different dried fruits or, in the summer, fresh fruits such as blueberries or blackberries. One tsp of blackstrap molasses adds extra nutrients and a lovely, rich flavour to the filling – but it's very sticky, so plan your baby's bath time for *after* he's eaten.
- For a similar dish that cooks in less time, use halved apples (or pears, nectarines or plums), laid face-down on a buttered ovenproof dish and covered in dried fruit, pre-soaked in a little apple or orange juice.

Warm Apple Wedges

These are great as first foods and dippers for little hands, but they also make a tasty snack or dessert for all ages. Use apples with plenty of flavour.

Serves as many as you wish

1 dessert or cooking apple per person
butter (preferably unsalted) for frying
a few pinches of ground cinnamon (optional)

Peel the apples, cut each one into 8–12 wedges and remove the core.

Heat the butter in a frying pan.

Sprinkle the apple wedges with cinnamon, if you like, and fry them very gently for about 15 minutes (depending on initial crunchiness) on all sides, turning as necessary, until just soft.

Lift the wedges onto kitchen paper to drain and cool slightly.

Serve warm on their own or with home-made custard (see page 161), natural yoghurt or crème fraîche.

Options

- Provided they are not overcooked (when they will be too soft), wedges make good dippers.
- Try mashing the wedges and spreading them on toast.
- Pear wedges also work well, so long as the pear is not too ripe.
- Try adding a few cloves to the oil to give a slightly different spicy flavour.

Rice Pudding

Rice pudding is a lovely, comforting dish that can be made with fruit purée, rather than lots of sugar, making it healthy, too. It's great practice for babies who are learning how to use a spoon, or it can be rolled into balls when cold for younger babies to get hold of.

Serves 2 adults and 1 baby

500ml (17½fl oz) milk

50g (2oz) pudding rice (short grain)

2 tbsp stewed fresh or dried fruit, blended to a purée (apricot, date, fig and mango are probably the sweetest; you can also use apple, blueberry, blackberry or pear)

1 tsp vanilla extract or 1 vanilla pod

Preheat the oven to 180°C/350°F/Gas Mark 4 and lightly grease an ovenproof dish.

Pour the milk into a saucepan and bring it to the boil. Stir in the rice and fruit purée, and the vanilla extract (if using).

Pour the mixture into the ovenproof dish. If using a vanilla pod, split it open with a knife, scrape out the seeds, and add both the seeds and the pod (don't forget to remove the pod before serving!).

Use a spoon to gently even out the rice throughout the dish. Don't worry that there seems to be very little rice – it expands as it's cooking.

Put the dish into the oven and bake for 15 minutes, then reduce the oven temperature to 150°C/300°F/Gas Mark 2 and bake for another 60–90 minutes, or until the rice has absorbed the milk and the pudding is golden on the top.

Serve warm, perhaps with some stewed fruit, but it is also delicious cold.

Options

- For a richer pudding, replace some of the milk with single cream.
- For a traditional rice pudding, replace the fruit purée with 25g (1oz) sugar.
- Try adding 50g (2oz) sultanas or chopped apricots to the mixture before pouring it into the ovenproof dish.
- Swap the vanilla for ½ tsp of ground cinnamon, or grate some nutmeg over the surface of the pudding just before it goes into the oven.

Fruit Crumble

This dish works well with any stewed fruit, although apple, blackberry and apple, and rhubarb are probably the 'classics'. Once your baby can get hold of handfuls of food and push or drop them into his mouth, he'll love this.

Serves 2 adults and 1 baby, twice

butter (preferably unsalted), for greasing
800–850g (1lb 12oz–1lb 14oz) fruit, stewed (see page 162)
100g (3½oz) self-raising flour
50g (2oz) butter (preferably unsalted)
25–50g (1–2oz) demerara sugar

Preheat the oven to 190°C/375°F/Gas Mark 5 and lightly grease an ovenproof dish.
   Drain the fruit of excess water or juice and place in the ovenproof dish.
   Sift the flour into a bowl. Cut or break the butter into small cubes and add it to the flour. Use your fingertips (or a pastry blender or food processor) to rub the butter into the flour until the mixture looks like fine breadcrumbs.
   Stir in the sugar, then sprinkle the crumble mixture over the fruit.
   Bake in the oven for 25–30 minutes, until the top is golden and crisp.
   Serve warm or cold, on its own, or with natural yoghurt, crème fraîche or home-made custard (see opposite).

Option

• Spices and/or dried fruit will give added flavour: a handful of raisins and a pinch of nutmeg goes well with apple (although not with blackberry and apple), cloves or a pinch of cinnamon with pears, and ginger with rhubarb. If you prefer to use cooking apples, you may need to add a little sugar to the fruit before baking, depending on taste. Rhubarb and some varieties of plums may also need a little sugar.

Home-made Custard

This beats custard made with custard powder hands down – it's better for you and it tastes better too. It contains a small amount of sugar but you can reduce this according to what you are serving it with.

300ml (11fl oz) full-fat milk
1 fresh vanilla pod, or 1 tsp real vanilla extract
2 large egg yolks
2 tsp cornflour
25g (1oz) caster sugar

Put the milk into a saucepan and heat gently until the milk is nearly boiling, then take the pan off the heat. Meanwhile, split the vanilla pod with a knife and take out the tiny seeds. Add both the seeds and the pod to the milk.

Whisk the egg yolks with the cornflour and sugar in a heatproof bowl until the mixture is thick and pale. If you are using vanilla extract, add this now. Pour the milk onto the egg mixture, stirring well. Discard the vanilla pod, if using, and return the mixture to the pan.

Return the pan to a low heat and stir continuously until the custard is thick enough to coat the back of a spoon. (This can take up to 8 minutes.)

Serve warm, poured over fruit, such as fresh bananas or peaches, or a sweet dessert such as stewed or baked fruit, fruit crumble or fruit pie.

Option

• If you want a more luxurious custard, use double or single cream in place of the milk.

Stewed Fruit

Stewed fruit makes a great dessert, especially in winter. Most fresh fruit is suitable for stewing; favourites are apples, pears, rhubarb, plums, blackberries and blackcurrants (bananas and citrus fruits don't stew well). Dried fruits (such as apricots, prunes and figs) can also be stewed, but unless they're labelled 'ready-to-eat' or 'pre-soaked' they need to be soaked overnight in cold water first. You may want to add about a teaspoon of caster sugar to some fruit, such as rhubarb, if it is too tart for your taste (although your baby might like it!). Fruits that are very ripe and sweet, and dried fruits, won't need any added sugar.

Note: Fruit should not be stewed in an aluminium or iron saucepan because these metals react with the acid in fruit juice.

Serves 2 adults and 1 baby

500g (1lb 2oz) fresh fruit or pre-soaked dried fruit
50ml (2fl oz) water
a little caster sugar, to taste (optional)

Wash, peel and cut up the fruit as necessary and put it into a saucepan. Add the water and the sugar (if using) and bring to the boil.

Turn down the heat, cover the pan and simmer until the fruit is soft (anything from 5–20 minutes, depending on the fruit). Check occasionally to make sure you can still see some water around the fruit – add more if necessary.

Serve warm or cold, with home-made custard (see overleaf), yoghurt, crème fraîche or yoghurt ice cream. If serving warm, test (by tasting) before offering the fruit to your baby, as some parts may remain very hot.

Options

• Try adding raisins, sultanas and/or nutmeg to apples during the cooking for a warmer flavour; a couple of cloves and a pinch of cinnamon (or a cinnamon stick) works well with pears; cinnamon is also good with plums, and ginger is good with rhubarb.
• You can also stew fruit in the microwave, in a covered dish with just a few tbsp of water. It will usually cook more quickly this way.

BREADS & BAKING

H ome baking is very satisfying and can be great fun – especially if you let your toddler help. Home-baked bread and cakes are much tastier than most shop-bought versions and they avoid the high salt and sugar levels of most baked goods sold in bakeries, supermarkets and cafés.

Bread-making

Baking your own bread isn't as time-consuming as it sounds and it gives you the advantage of knowing exactly what is in it, plus the chance to experiment with different ingredients. If you don't have time to knead traditional dough, or to wait for it to rise, you can make a delicious loaf of Easy Bread (see page 166) very quickly.

Your own home-baked bread will almost certainly be healthier than commercial bread – although most people find it's too bland without any salt. For adults, using salted butter or a salty spread will make salt-free bread tastier, but you may want to add up to 1 tsp of salt to the recipe (this will also help the bread to keep longer).

The key to baking successfully with yeast is gentle warmth – warm water, warm hands and a warm place for the dough to rise. It's almost impossible to 'hurt' dough, so feel free to channel all your energy and frustrations into the kneading – the more vigorous it is, the better.

When shaping your dough, remember that large, solid loaves take longer to cook, and need a slower (cooler) oven than small or flat loaves or rolls.

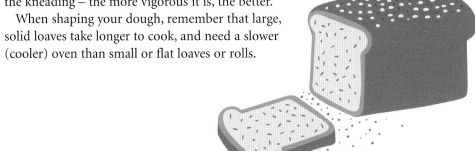

Basic Bread

This recipe is for bread made by hand. You may need to adapt the ingredients (for example, by adding less water) if you are using a breadmaking machine.

Makes 1 large loaf or 12 rolls (see page 166)

15g (½oz) fresh yeast or 1½ tsp dried yeast (or according to the packet's instructions) with 1 tsp sugar (caster sugar works best)

450g (1lb) strong bread flour (half-white, half-wholemeal is good), plus extra for dusting

½–1 tsp salt (optional)

1–2 tbsp oil (optional, but it will help the bread to stay moist), plus extra for greasing

250–300ml (9–11fl oz) warm (not hot) water

If using dried yeast, follow the packet instructions.

Put the flour and the salt (if using) into a large bowl and make a well in the centre. Pour in the oil and add the yeast (or yeast/sugar mixture).

Mix to a smooth, elastic dough, adding some water as necessary. (If it ends up too sticky, just add a little more flour.) A slightly softer mixture is okay for baking in a tin; if you are going to shape the dough on a baking sheet it will need to be slightly stiffer.

Place the dough on a lightly floured surface and knead vigorously for 5–10 minutes by pulling the outside of the dough into the centre with your fingers, then pushing it out again with your knuckles, and turning it over now and then. (First kneading.)

Put the dough back in the bowl, cover it with cling film or a clean, damp tea towel (to stop a skin forming) and leave it in a warm place for at least 45 minutes until it has doubled in size and springs back when you press it with a finger.

Lightly grease a 1kg (2lb) loaf tin or a baking sheet.

Take the dough out of the bowl, punch it a few times to knock out the air and knead it again for a couple of minutes. (Second kneading.)

Shape the loaf and put it into the tin or on to the baking sheet.

Cover as before and leave to 'prove' (i.e. rise for a second time). This usually takes about 20–30 minutes. Meanwhile, preheat the oven to 220°C/425°F/Gas Mark 7.

When the loaf has risen, put it in the oven and bake for 30–40 minutes.

Turn the loaf out to cool on a wire rack.

Alternative quick method

If you are in a hurry, you can make bread with just one kneading and rising, although the finished loaf may not be quite as light. Just follow the instructions opposite, then, after one bout of vigorous kneading, shape the loaf and put it into the tin or on to the baking sheet. Leave it to rise until it has doubled in size (about 45 minutes) and then put it into a preheated oven.

Options

- You can experiment with different bread flours, such as granary or spelt, or a combination of flours. A loaf made with half-white, half-wholemeal flour has some of the goodness of the wholegrain but is lighter than wholemeal bread. Ordinary plain flour can be used with reasonable results, but special ('strong') bread flour works best.
- Using milk instead of water gives a sweeter loaf; using melted butter (preferably unsalted) instead of oil makes it richer.
- Try rolling your loaf in sunflower seeds (or similar) before the second rising, or sprinkling poppy seeds on top just before baking, to give a crust with extra texture and flavour. (Crush any seeds that may be difficult for your baby to manage before adding them.)
- You can adapt this basic bread recipe to make a variety of tasty loaves or rolls, just by adding extra ingredients when you are mixing the dough. Here are some to try: 100g (3½oz) finely grated cheese and a pinch of freshly ground black pepper; 2 tbsp sun-dried tomatoes (chopped), with 1 tsp dried mixed herbs; 2 tbsp finely chopped onion; 2 tbsp crushed sunflower or pumpkin seeds (or poppy or sesame seeds).
- For fruit bread, replace the oil and water with melted (but not hot) butter (preferably unsalted) and warm milk, and add approx 75g (2½oz) dried fruit, such as raisins, sultanas, dried apricots (chopped) or cranberries (together with 1 tsp ground cinnamon, if you like a spicy flavour). The top can be brushed with warm milk halfway through baking to give a rich, glossy finish.

Storage: Yeast doughs can be kept in the fridge for a few days, or frozen for up to three months. Just punch the air out of the dough after the first rising, wrap it in cling-film and put it in the freezer. You will need to bring it back to a warm room temperature before kneading it for the second time and baking it. Baked loaves and rolls (see page 166) can also be frozen, but only for about a month, or the crust will start to break away.

Bread Rolls

Follow the recipe for basic bread (see page 164), using slightly less water so that you have a stiffer mixture.

After the second kneading (or the first, if you are in a hurry), lightly grease a baking sheet, then cut the dough into about 12 pieces.

Shape the pieces into rolls and space them at least 5cm (2in) apart on the baking sheet.

Cover with cling film or a clean damp tea towel and leave to prove (rise) until roughly doubled in size.

Heat the oven to 230°C/450°F/Gas Mark 8. Bake the bread rolls for about 15 minutes.

Option

• The options at the end of the basic bread recipe also work for bread rolls.

Easy Bread

This simple soda bread is quick to make and absolutely delicious, especially fresh from the oven with a little butter. It requires no kneading or rising – the ingredients are simply combined and then popped into the oven, resulting in a lovely rustic loaf.

Makes a 500g (1lb 2oz) loaf

250g (9oz) self-raising flour, plus extra for dusting
250g (9oz) wholemeal flour
½ tsp baking powder
½ tsp bicarbonate of soda
pinch of salt (optional)
450–500g (1lb 2oz) live (pro-biotic) natural yoghurt

Preheat the oven to 180°C/350°F/Gas Mark 4 and prepare a floured baking sheet.

Sift the flours, baking powder, bicarbonate of soda and salt (if using) into a bowl and make a well in the centre. Pour in the yoghurt and combine with the flour to make a dough. If it's too sticky, add a little more flour.

Shape the dough into a ball, put it on to the floured baking sheet and flatten slightly. Bake in the oven for 50–60 minutes, then transfer to a wire rack to cool.

Tortillas and Chapattis

Flat breads, such as Mexican flour tortillas and Indian chapattis, are often easier for babies to handle than breads that have risen. They are usually cooked in a dry pan rather than in the oven and are very quick to make (most recipes suggest 'resting' the dough before cooking, but it's not essential). They're made with ordinary flour rather than strong 'bread' flour, and you can use oil or butter instead of the traditional lard.

Makes 10–15 tortillas (or chapattis)

> *for tortillas:* 450g (1lb) plain flour, plus 1 tsp baking powder
> *for chapattis:* 450g (1lb) wholemeal flour, or half-wholemeal, half-white
> a little extra flour for dusting
> 25g (1oz) lard (unhydrogenated) or butter (preferably unsalted), cut into cubes and softened, or 2 tbsp oil
> about 275ml (9fl oz) warm water

Sift the flour (and baking powder, for tortillas) into a large bowl and make a well in the centre. If using lard or butter, roughly rub it into the flour; if using oil, just mix it straight in. Gradually add approx 275ml (9½fl oz) water (you may not need it all), mixing until the dough holds together. (If it ends up too sticky, just add a little more flour.)

Place the dough on a floured surface and knead for 5 minutes until smooth and springy. Divide the dough into 10–15 balls, depending on how large you want your tortillas or chapattis to be. Cover them and allow them to rest for 10–15 minutes.

Preheat a large, dry, flat griddle or frying pan over a Medium–High heat.

Using a well-floured rolling pin and a floured surface, flatten one ball into a thin, round shape, rolling away from you and turning the dough (or the board) once or twice. If you want to use the tortilla/chapatti as a wrap, the thinner you get it, the easier it will be to roll up once it's cooked.

Lightly flour the tortilla/chapatti and place it in the hot pan. Cook for 45–60 seconds until it has a papery feel and the underside is speckled brown, then flip it over and cook the other side for about 30 seconds. As you cook them, stack the cooked breads on a warm plate covered with a clean tea towel to keep them soft. You should just about have time to roll out the next tortilla or chapatti while the current one is cooking!

Serve warm or cold, with a filling of your choice, or a curry or dahl.

Cheese Straws

These delicious, crumbly sticks are great for taking out, and they can be made into the perfect shape and size for your baby to hold – though he will need some practice to discover how to handle them without crushing them. Cheese straws can be eaten on their own or with a dip such as Hummus (see page 73).

Makes 12–15 straws

50g (2oz) unsalted butter, plus extra for greasing
100g (3½oz) plain flour, plus extra for dusting
50–75g (2–2½oz) cheese, grated, to taste
1 egg, beaten
a little cold water (if needed)

Preheat the oven to 200°C/400°F/Gas Mark 6 and lightly grease a baking sheet.

Put the flour into a bowl. Cut or break the butter into small cubes and add it to the flour. Using your hands, a pastry blender or a food processor, rub the butter into the flour until the mixture looks like fine breadcrumbs.

Stir in the cheese and mix well, then make a well in the centre. Pour in the egg and stir until the mixture begins to form a dough, adding a little water, if necessary, to hold it together.

Place the dough on a floured surface and knead it with your fingertips for a few minutes until the ingredients are evenly mixed. Roll the dough into thick pencil shapes 10–15cm (4–6in) long and place them about 2cm (¾in) apart on the baking sheet. Bake for about 10 minutes, until pale golden in colour.

Remove from the oven and allow to cool slightly before transferring to a wire rack to finish cooling.

'When Charlie got older and had stopped breastfeeding, his behaviour would go downhill mid-morning and mid-afternoon. I didn't realise that he just needed a snack twice a day.'

Jan, mother of Charlie, 3 years

English Muffins

Traditional English muffins are slightly richer than bread and make a great alternative to hamburger buns or toast.

Makes about 12 muffins

225ml (8fl oz) milk

15g (½oz) fresh yeast or 1½–2 tsp dried yeast with 1 tsp sugar (caster sugar works best)

450g (1lb) strong flour, plus extra for dusting

½–1 tsp salt (optional)

oil or butter (preferably unsalted) for frying

Put the milk into a pan and heat gently until it is lukewarm. Pour a little into a small bowl and stir in the yeast. If using dried yeast, follow the packet instructions.

Sift the flour and salt (if using) into a large bowl and make a well in the centre. Pour in the yeast mixture and the rest of the milk, and mix to form a dough. It should feel soft and dry; if it doesn't, add a little more warm milk (to make it softer) or flour (if you need it drier) until you get the right consistency.

Place the dough on a lightly floured surface and knead for about 10 minutes, until it is smooth and elastic. Put the dough back in the bowl, cover it with cling film or a clean, damp tea towel and leave it in a warm place for at least 45 minutes until it has doubled in size and springs back when you press it with a finger.

Take the dough out of the bowl, punch it a few times to knock out the air and knead it again briefly. Then, using a rolling pin, roll it out to about 1cm (½in) thick.

Using a 7.5cm (3in) pastry cutter, cut out as many rounds as you can, kneading the scraps together and re-rolling the dough as needed. Place the muffins on a floured surface and leave them in a warm place for 25–35 minutes to rise.

When the muffins are puffy, heat a flat griddle or large frying pan (preferably non-stick), with a very thin coating of oil or butter, over a medium heat. Put a few of the muffins on to the griddle or into the pan and turn the heat down low. Cook for about 7 minutes, then turn them over and cook for another 7 minutes.

Serve warm, toasted lightly on both sides, then split in half. Spread with unsalted butter and a sweet or savoury topping of your choice.

Simple Scones

These simple, egg-free scones are lovely warm or cold. They are quite dense so are easy for younger babies to grasp without crushing. Savoury versions go well with Guacamole (see page 74), Hummus (see page 73), cream cheese or Bean Spread (see page 75). Plain or fruit scones are great with crème fraîche or cream and jam (or fruit spread).

Makes about 8 scones

225g (8oz) self-raising flour (or 225g/8oz plain flour with 3 tsp baking powder)
1 tsp baking powder
50g (2oz) butter (preferably unsalted)
approx 150ml (5fl oz) milk

Preheat the oven to 220°C/425°F/Gas Mark 7 and lightly grease a baking sheet. Put the flour and baking powder together into a bowl. Cut or break the butter into small cubes and add it to the flour. Using your hands, a pastry blender or a food processor, rub the butter into the flour until the mixture looks like fine breadcrumbs.

Make a well in the centre of the mixture and pour in a little of the milk.

Gently fold the dry mixture into the milk and work them together, adding more milk until you have a dough that is soft but not sticky.

On a floured board, knead the dough a little, then roll or gently press it out, so that it is about 2cm (¾in) thick. Cut into round or triangular scones (you can use a biscuit cutter or an upside-down cup for round ones).

Place the scones on the baking sheet, about 2cm (¾in) apart. Bake for 10–15 minutes, then cool on a wire rack.

Serve warm or cold.

Options

- Extra ingredients can be added to the mixture, after you've rubbed in the butter and before you add the milk. For fruit scones, try 50g (2oz) raisins, sultanas, or chopped dates or dried apricots. For savoury scones, try 75–100g (2½–3½oz) cooked mashed potato, sweet potato, swede or butternut squash – with ½ tsp dried herbs (or 1½ tsp fresh herbs).
- For cheese scones, add 75–100g (2½–3½oz) grated cheese.

Muffins

Muffins can be sweet or savoury and are usually a big hit with both babies and older children – you'll probably find you are still making them for lunchboxes and picnics when your baby is at school!

A gentle folding technique is used for combining the wet and dry ingredients, as it encourages plenty of air to stay in the mixture, making the muffins nice and light.

Muffins are best baked in a muffin tray (deeper than a fairy cake tray). Lining it with paper cases makes the muffins easier to tip out and helps to stop them breaking up when packed to take out with you. The cooking time is approximate – the muffins should be baked until they are golden brown and springy. If you're not sure whether they are done, heat a skewer and gently push it into the centre of one of the muffins in the middle of the tray; it should be clean when you pull it out. If there is anything stuck to it, the muffins are not quite ready. If the outside of the muffins begins to burn before the insides are cooked, reduce the temperature of your oven.

The following recipes are for regular-sized muffins but you may prefer to make smaller ones, so that they are easier for little hands to hold. Smaller muffins will take less time to cook.

Banana Muffins

This tasty sugar-free recipe is a great way to use up bananas that have got a bit too ripe.

Makes 12 regular-sized muffins

150g (5½oz) self-raising flour (white, wholemeal or half-and-half)
½ tsp ground cinnamon, nutmeg or mixed spice (optional)
60g (2oz) butter (preferably unsalted), plus extra for greasing
4 large, very ripe bananas
2 large eggs, beaten

Preheat the oven to 190°C/375°F/Gas Mark 5 and lightly grease a muffin tray or line with paper cases.

Sift the flour and spices into a large bowl and make a well in the centre.

Melt the butter in a small pan over a low heat.

In a separate bowl, mash the bananas to a smooth, thick purée consistency using a fork or a potato masher. Add the eggs and melted butter and mix well.

Pour the banana mixture into the flour and fold together lightly, then spoon the mixture into the muffin tray.

Bake for 10–15 minutes (depending on size), until golden brown and springy, then remove from the oven and allow to cool for a few minutes before turning out.

> **Tip:** *Instead of throwing away over-ripe bananas, put them in the freezer ready for the next time you make this recipe.*

Option

- If you like you can add a handful of sultanas or finely chopped dates with the banana mixture.

Carrot Muffins

These muffins are surprisingly sweet, and perfect when you want a lighter muffin.

Makes about 10 regular-sized muffins

150g (5½oz) self-raising flour (white, wholemeal or half-and-half)
60g (2oz) butter (preferably unsalted), plus extra for greasing
2 large eggs, beaten
2 medium carrots, grated
3–4 tbsp milk
zest of 2 oranges, juice of 1 (optional)

Preheat the oven to 190°C/375°F/Gas Mark 5 and lightly grease a muffin tray or line with paper cases.

Sift the flour into a large bowl and make a well in the centre.

Melt the butter in a small pan over a low heat. In a separate bowl, combine the eggs and grated carrot, then add the melted butter and mix well. Pour the carrot mixture into the flour and fold together lightly.

Add enough milk to give a soft consistency, then spoon the mixture into the muffin tray.

Bake for 10–15 minutes (depending on size), until golden brown and springy, then remove from the oven and allow to cool for a few minutes before turning out.

Cheese and Spinach Muffins

Savoury muffins make great snacks and are easy for babies to eat.

Makes 10 regular-sized muffins

oil or butter (preferably unsalted) for frying, plus extra butter
　for greasing
½ small red onion, finely chopped
175g (6oz) plain flour
1½ tsp baking powder
1 tsp cayenne pepper
1 egg
110ml (4fl oz) milk
125g (4½oz) grated cheese
60–75g (2–2½oz) baby spinach leaves, torn

Preheat the oven to 160°C/325°F/Gas Mark 3. Heat the oil or butter in a frying pan, add the onion and fry until soft, then lift it out using a slotted spoon (to drain off the oil) and set aside.

Sift the flour, baking powder and cayenne pepper into a bowl and make a well in the centre. Beat the egg in a jug or bowl and add the milk, whisking them together, then pour the mixture into the flour and fold together.

Add the cheese, fried onion and spinach, and fold gently until evenly mixed, then spoon the mixture into the muffin tray.

Bake for 15–20 minutes (depending on size), until golden brown and springy, then remove from the oven and allow to cool in the muffin tray for a few minutes before turning out.

'Levi doesn't really like sandwiches; he just dismantles them. So we take out savoury muffins or cheese scones for a packed lunch or a big snack. They are easy to make and good to freeze, so we've always got some.'

Ruth, mother of Levi, 19 months

Extra-healthy Sweet Muffins

These muffins are delicious, sugar-free and packed with healthy ingredients. Grind the nuts unless you are sure your baby can manage them chopped.

Makes 12 regular-sized muffins

butter (preferably unsalted), for greasing

2 eggs, beaten

100ml (3½fl oz) sunflower oil

1 tsp vanilla extract

225g (8oz) wholemeal self-raising flour (or half-white, half-wholemeal)

2 medium carrots, grated

2 dessert apples, peeled, cored and grated

75–100g (2½–3½oz) dates, finely chopped

50g (2oz) desiccated coconut

50g (2oz) pecan nuts or walnuts, ground or finely chopped (optional)

½ tsp ground cinnamon

½ tsp nutmeg

Preheat the oven to 180°C/350°F/Gas Mark 4 and lightly grease a muffin tray or line with paper cases.

Put the eggs, oil and vanilla into a bowl and mix well. Sift the flour into another bowl and add the carrots, apples, dates, coconut, nuts and spices. Stir briefly, then make a well in the centre. Add the egg mixture and fold together lightly.

Spoon the mixture into the muffin tray and bake for 15–25 minutes (depending on size), until golden brown and springy, then remove from the oven and allow to cool for a few minutes before turning out.

Option

• For older children, roughly chopping the nuts will give a lovely texture.

Savoury Flapjacks

Flapjacks are excellent for picnics and long journeys, being less crumbly and more filling than either scones or muffins. Oats also provide a break from wheat and are very nutritious.

Ordinary rolled porridge oats (not 'instant' oat cereal) usually work better for flapjacks than jumbo oats, which tend to break up when baked and may make the flapjack too crumbly for your baby to manage easily. A Swiss roll tin (approx 20 x 32cm (18 x 12½in) and 2cm (¾in) deep) is ideal for making flapjacks.

> **100g (3½oz) butter (preferably unsalted), plus extra for greasing**
> **300g (10½oz) porridge oats**
> **350g (12½oz) cheese, grated**
> **2 eggs, beaten**

Preheat the oven to 180°C/350°F/Gas Mark 4 and lightly grease a Swiss roll tin.

Melt the butter in a small pan over a low heat. Combine all the ingredients in the pan off the heat and mix well. Press the mixture into the greased tin using the back of a spoon (it should be about 1cm/½in thick) and bake in the oven for 20 minutes until golden brown.

Allow to cool in the tin for 5 minutes, then cut into slices and cool on a wire rack.

Option

• You can also add vegetables to this basic recipe, which will give you a lighter flapjack with extra flavours. Try adding 200–300g (7–10½oz) of one of the following (grated): carrot, courgette, red onion, sweet potato, swede or parsnip.

Baked Oat Cake

This tasty, moist cake contains no added sugar – the sweetness comes from the fruit and the cinnamon. If you don't have any oatmeal, just whizz up some porridge oats in a blender or food processor.

2 tbsp oil, plus extra for greasing

1 large apple with plenty of flavour

approx 80g (3oz) raisins or other dried fruit

few pinches of ground cinnamon

1–2 tbsp water

200g (7oz) oatmeal

1 tsp baking powder

220ml (7½fl oz) milk

1 egg, beaten

Preheat the oven to 180°C/350°F/Gas Mark 4 and lightly grease a 500g (1lb) loaf tin.

Peel, core and slice the apple and put it into a small pan with the raisins, a pinch of cinnamon and the water. Cook gently for about 10 minutes, until the apple is soft, then mash it and mix well with the raisins.

Put all the other ingredients into a bowl and mix well. Add the apple and raisin mixture and combine.

Pour the mixture into the loaf tin and sprinkle cinnamon on the top. Bake in the oven for about 30 minutes. (Insert a skewer to check that it's cooked – it should come out clean.)

Remove from the oven and allow to cool in the tin before turning out and cutting into wedges.

Serve warm or cold, but the cake is easier to cut if allowed to cool first.

Options

- If you want a smoother cake, blend the mixture with an electric blender before putting it into the loaf tin.
- You can pre-cook the apple and raisins in the microwave, rather than a pan.
- This cake is also delicious with a mashed ripe banana, added along with the apple.

Sugar-free Carrot Cake

The sweetness in this lovely cake comes from the carrots, dates, coconut and spices. Grind the nuts unless you are sure your baby can manage them chopped.

200g (7oz) wholemeal self-raising flour and 1 tsp baking powder
(or 200g/7oz plain flour with 3 tsp baking powder)
110g (4oz) dates, finely chopped
50g (2oz) desiccated coconut
50g (2oz) nuts (e.g. walnuts or mixed nuts), finely chopped or
ground
3 tsp ground mixed spice, cinnamon or nutmeg
110g (4oz) melted butter (preferably unsalted)
110g (4oz) sultanas
1 large carrot, grated
grated zest of 1 orange and 2 tbsp orange juice
2 eggs, beaten

For the topping (optional):
200g (7oz) cream cheese (mascarpone works well)
100g (3½oz) dates, finely chopped
zest and juice of 1 orange or lemon (unwaxed)

Preheat the oven to 150°C/300°F/Gas Mark 2 and lightly grease a (deep) 20cm (8in) round cake tin. Sift the flour and baking powder into a large bowl and add the dates, coconut, nuts and spices. Mix thoroughly, then make a well in the centre.

Combine the melted butter, sultanas, carrot and orange zest and juice. Add to the dry ingredients and combine to make a thick paste. Add the eggs and mix thoroughly.

Spoon the mixture into the cake tin and place in the oven. Bake for 45–60 minutes, or until done. (Check by inserting a skewer – it should come out clean.)

Remove from the oven and allow to cool for 5–10 minutes, then turn out on to a wire rack to finish cooling. If using the topping, blend the ingredients until smooth and spread over the cake. Alternatively, serve with mascarpone or whipped cream.

Banana Cake

Banana cake is deliciously moist and sweet. It's best made with bananas that are really over-ripe – the more they ripen, the sweeter they become, so don't throw those squishy ones away!

butter or oil for greasing

100g (3½oz) self-raising wholemeal flour (or 100g/3½oz plain
    flour with 2 tsp baking powder)

½ tsp ground mixed spice

50g (2oz) butter (preferably unsalted)

75g (2½oz) raisins (or chopped figs)

200g (7oz) mashed banana (1½–2 medium-sized ripe bananas)

50g (2oz) walnuts, ground or finely chopped (optional)

1 egg, beaten

For the topping (optional):
200g (7oz) cream cheese
50–100g (2–3½oz) 100% fruit spread or jam (optional)

Preheat the oven to 180°C/350°F/Gas Mark 4 and lightly grease a 450g (1lb) loaf tin.

Sift the flour into a large bowl and add the spices. Cut or break the butter into small cubes and add it to the flour. Using your hands, a pastry blender or a food processor, rub the butter into the flour until the mixture looks like fine bread-crumbs. Stir in the raisins (or figs) and make a well in the centre of the mixture.

In a separate bowl, mash the banana, add the walnuts (if using) and stir in the egg. Pour the banana mixture into the flour mixture and fold in.

Put the mixture into the loaf tin and put it in the oven. Turn the oven down to 160°C/325°F/Gas Mark 3 and bake for 45–60 minutes, or until done. (Check by inserting a skewer – it should come out clean.)

Remove the tin from the oven and allow to cool for 5–10 minutes, then turn out on to a wire rack to finish cooling.

Serve plain, with crème fraîche or natural yoghurt, or covered with the topping. To make the topping, combine the ingredients and mix thoroughly (using a blender or food processor if the jam is lumpy), then spread evenly over the cake.

Spanish Apple Cake

This delicious, moist cake has plenty of fruit in it and is quick and easy to make, using olive oil rather than butter.

> **250g (9oz) self-raising flour**
> **½ tsp cinnamon**
> **50g (2oz) caster sugar**
> **juice and zest of 1 unwaxed lemon**
> **2 eggs, beaten**
> **160ml (5½fl oz) olive oil**
> **450g (1lb) crisp dessert apples**

Preheat the oven to 180°C/350°F/Gas Mark 4.

Sift the flour and cinnamon into a large bowl and add the sugar and lemon zest.

Make a well in the centre and add the eggs, olive oil and lemon juice, stirring as you go, to make a smooth mixture.

Peel, core and chop the apples into roughly 2cm (1in) cubes. Fold them gently into the cake mixture and pour everything into a lightly greased 17cm (7in) round cake tin.

Oven bake for 40–45 minutes until firm to the touch in the centre and golden brown on top.

Leave the cake to cool slightly in the tin for a few minutes, then turn out on to a wire rack.

Serve cold as a snack, or warm with cream or home-made custard (see page 161) .

Option

• You can swap the cinnamon for nutmeg, or use crisp pears instead of apples.

Basic Techniques & Recipes

I t's really useful to have a few basic techniques up your sleeve that can be used to make different dishes. Making your own pastry, stocks and sauces will provide the basis of a whole range of meals, and means you can choose ingredients that are healthy for your baby.

Pastry

Pastry can be made with butter, a mixture of butter and (unhydrogenated) lard, or for a healthier version, olive (or sunflower) oil. The key to making mouth-watering pastry is to keep things light and cool, and to handle the dough as little as possible. Use cold water and, if you are making pastry by hand, try to have cool hands, too. Lifting your hands as you gently rub in the fat will keep the mixture light. If you prefer, you can use a pastry blender or a food processor for the rubbing in, but the kneading, which should be very brief, is best done by hand.

Storage: *Uncooked pastry dough can be kept in the fridge for a couple of days, wrapped in food-safe cling film. Both uncooked and cooked pastry freeze well, wrapped tightly.*

   When rolling pastry (and other doughs), roll away from you, pressing downwards more than outwards. This will help to stop the dough shrinking while it cooks. Roll on a floured surface and turn the dough round, so you can keep rolling in the same direction – or use a board and turn the board. There is no need to flip the dough over but you should lift it up occasionally to check that it is not sticking to the board.

Simple Shortcrust Pastry

This recipe makes enough pastry to line a 23cm (9in) pie dish or tin; if you want to make a pie with a lid, you will need about 1½ times these quantities. When recipes ask for 250g pastry, this means pastry made with 250g (9oz) flour, as in this recipe.

125g (4½oz) fat – butter (preferably unsalted), or half-lard (unhydrogenated) and half-butter, plus extra for greasing
250g (9oz) plain flour, plus extra for dusting
about 3 tbsp cold water to bind

Lightly grease the pie dish or tin. Put the flour into a bowl and add the fat (cut or broken into small cubes), then use your fingertips to rub the fat into the flour until the mixture looks like fine breadcrumbs. Using a cold blunt knife, stir in the water a few drops at a time with a criss-crossing cutting motion. Stop when the mixture starts to clump together. Gather the mixture into one lump and knead it lightly for a few seconds, using your fingertips only, until it forms a stiff dough.

Place the pastry on a lightly floured surface and roll it gently until it is about 3mm (⅛in) thick. Then lift it carefully (by laying it over the rolling pin) and transfer it to your pie dish or tin. Shape the pastry to fit, easing it gently into any corners rather than stretching it. Bake the pastry blind (see below) if you like, then fill and cook according to the recipe instructions.

Options

- You can make pastry with oil, instead of butter or lard. Olive oil is best for savoury dishes, and sunflower oil is better for sweet dishes. Just replace the fat with 65ml (2½fl oz) of oil, mixed into the flour with a fork (or electric mixer) until the mixture is crumbly and moist. Gradually add approx 125ml (4fl oz) cold water, until the mixture starts to clump together, then follow the recipe as above.
- To make cheese pastry, use 200g (7oz) plain flour, 100g (3½oz) fat and 100g (3½oz) grated cheese. Add the cheese after you've rubbed the fat into the flour.

How to bake a pastry case 'blind'

Baking a pastry case 'blind' (i.e. with nothing in it) is a way of making sure that the bottom of your pie or quiche doesn't end up soggy. It's especially useful when the filling is very wet or doesn't need to cook for long, so it's good for fruit tarts and quiches.

181

To keep the bottom of the case flat and to prevent trapped air pushing it up, you can either prick the base in several places with a fork, or line it with greaseproof paper and weight it down with a layer of ceramic baking beans, or dried beans, lentils or rice.

Put the pastry case into a preheated oven (190°C/375°F/Gas Mark 5) and cook for 10–12 minutes. Check to make sure it's beginning to look dry (but not browned) and remove the beans and paper (if used). If you like, brush the inside with a little beaten egg to keep the base crisp, then put it back into the oven for another 3–5 minutes to finish cooking. Once it's baked, if there are any cracks or holes in the pastry, patch them with off-cuts of raw pastry before adding your filling.

STOCKS

A good stock is the basis of many soups, sauces and other dishes, giving much more flavour to the dish than if you simply used water. Ready-made stock cubes tend to contain a lot of salt, so if you have the time, making your own is a much better option when you have young children. It's also a great way to use 'tired' vegetables or the bones from a roast chicken.

Stock is ideal for making in batches and freezing. Large, empty yoghurt pots or 250–500ml (9–17½fl oz) containers are ideal for this. To use the stock, thaw it in the fridge or put the frozen lump into a pan and bring it to the boil before using it.

Although you can add lots of ingredients and seasonings when you make stock, if you are making it in batches and don't yet know what you are going to use it for, keep it simple and add herbs, garlic, etc., later, according to the eventual recipe.

Simple Meat or Chicken Stock

Meat or chicken stock is made from bones, which are full of flavour. Using a chicken carcass or the bone from a leg of lamb to make stock will mean you get all the goodness out of it (it will also loosen any remaining meat, so you can save that too). Alternatively, you can buy bones on their own from a butcher specifically for making stock. Ask him or her to chop them into usable-sized pieces for you.

The most basic stock uses just meat bones but you can add a few root vegetables – such as carrots or turnips (but not potato, because it disintegrates when cooked for long periods) – or the stalks of other vegetables, such as broccoli or cauliflower to give a little more flavour.

500g (1lb 2oz) meat bones (lamb, beef, pork or venison), or
the bones (carcass) from a whole chicken (including any
remaining skin)
1 litre (1¾ pint) cold water
1 celery stick
5–10 black peppercorns (optional)

Put the bones into a large pan. (If using a chicken carcass, break it up as necessary so that it fits snugly into the pan.) Add approx 1 litre (1¾ pints) cold water, ensuring that the bones are covered, and bring to the boil.

Cut the celery into fairly large pieces. When the water in the pan has boiled, skim any scum off the surface of the liquid, add the celery and peppercorns and bring back to the boil. Skim again if necessary, then reduce the heat, cover and simmer for about 3 hours.

Strain the stock through a sieve to remove all the solid bits and allow it to cool. Skim off the excess fat, then refrigerate or freeze the stock until you want to use it.

Simple Vegetable Stock

Vegetable stock is made by simmering vegetables until they have given up most of their flavour to the surrounding water. The vegetables are then thrown away. If you want to make a soup that includes vegetables, you will need to use fresh vegetables, rather than those that were used to make the stock. This recipe needs a 3 litre (5 pint) pan.

400g (14 oz) (approx 3 large) onions
400g (14 oz) (approx 6 medium-sized) carrots
4–5 celery sticks
1 small turnip
5–10 black peppercorns (optional)

Cut the vegetables into fairly large pieces and put into a large pan. Add the peppercorns (if using) and 2½ litres (5¼ pints) water and bring to the boil. Reduce the heat, cover and simmer for about 3 hours.

Strain the stock through a colander to remove all the solid bits and allow it to cool. Refrigerate or freeze the stock until you want to use it.

OTHER BASIC RECIPES

Classic Basil Pesto

Having a jar of pesto in the fridge can be a life saver if you are in a hurry – simply cook up some pasta, add pesto and you have a tasty meal. It is also great with fish, and adds an extra flavour to soups (add just before serving), sandwiches, roasted vegetables and many other dishes.

Most shop-bought versions of pesto contain salt but it's easy to make your own and it keeps well in the fridge. This is a very tasty version, with a good texture; it can be made in a pestle and mortar (if you want to be traditional), or in a food processor (if you're in a hurry).

The amounts of cheese, pine nuts and oil can be varied according to taste. It's probably best to avoid Chinese and Korean pine nuts as occasionally they leave a bitter aftertaste.

> 1 large bunch fresh basil (about a mugful when chopped)
> 1–2 garlic cloves, finely chopped or crushed
> 30g (1oz) pine nuts
> 50g (2oz) Parmesan cheese, freshly grated
> 25g (1oz) Pecorino cheese, freshly grated (or another
>   25g/1oz Parmesan)
> approx 100ml (3½fl oz) olive oil
> pinch of ground black pepper (optional)

Pestle and mortar method

Roughly chop the basil leaves and pound in a large mortar with the chopped garlic.

Crush the pine nuts between sheets of greaseproof or waxed paper with a rolling pin (optional, but it saves time). Add the pine nuts to the mortar and grind the mixture thoroughly until you have a thick paste.

Add the cheeses and pound again. Add the olive oil a little at a time, testing for preferred texture, then add a pinch of black pepper if desired, and grind or pound again.

Allow the pesto to stand for 5 minutes before serving.

Food processor method

Combine the basil, garlic and cheese and blend.

Add the nuts and blend again briefly.

Keep blending and slowly add the olive oil, checking the consistency as you go. Don't aim for complete smoothness – it should have some texture. Transfer the mixture to a bowl and add black pepper to taste.

Allow the pesto to stand for 5 minutes before serving.

Options

- For an extra-nutty flavour, toast the pine nuts slightly beforehand by warming them for a few minutes in a dry frying pan.
- If you like, you can use walnuts or cashew nuts instead of pine nuts.
- Add a little lemon juice at the end, for an extra kick.
- You can use rocket – or even watercress – instead of basil.

Quick Curry Paste

This basic mild curry paste will keep in the fridge for a couple of weeks. It's made with ready-ground spices, but, if you have an electric grinder (or a large pestle and mortar and plenty of time), you can start with whole coriander and cumin seeds for a more authentic version. (Remember to wash your hands after handling raw chilli, and before touching your baby because chilli juice can sting.)

1 fresh mild/medium chilli pepper (deseeded, veins removed), finely chopped

5–6 garlic cloves, finely chopped or crushed

2cm (¾in) piece of fresh ginger, grated

4 tbsp ground coriander seeds

4 tbsp ground cumin seeds

2 tbsp mustard seeds, crushed

1 tbsp chilli powder

1 tbsp turmeric

1 tbsp paprika

olive oil

Finely chop the chilli pepper. Add the garlic and ginger (and any juices) and grind until fairly smooth. Add the spices and grind again. Add enough oil to make a soft paste.

Transfer the paste to a jar and put it in the fridge.

Mild Thai Green Curry Paste

Recipes such as Thai green fish or chicken curry call for Thai green curry paste. Shop-bought varieties tend to be very hot, as do many recipes for home-made versions. This is a milder version but it's still quite hot, so you may want to offer your baby a tiny amount and include plenty of mild coconut milk in your curry to start with. Alternatively, you could use a little less chilli. The paste will keep for about a week in an airtight jar in the fridge. (Remember to wash your hands after handling the raw chilli, and before touching your baby because chilli juice can sting.)

> 2 mild/medium green chilli peppers (deseeded and veins
>   removed)
> 2 shallots (or 4 spring onions)
> 3 garlic cloves
> 2–3cm (¾–1¼in) piece of fresh ginger, peeled
> 2 lemongrass stalks, trimmed, outer leaves discarded and
>   chopped
> 2 tbsp fresh coriander, chopped
> 1 tsp ground cumin
> 1 tsp ground coriander seeds
> 1 tsp grated lime zest (unwaxed)
> 1 tbsp lime juice
> 2 tbsp oil (if needed)

Finely chop the chilli peppers, shallots, garlic and ginger by hand or using a food processor. Add the other ingredients and blend thoroughly until smooth (use a pestle and mortar for a really smooth paste). Add a little oil, if needed, to give a manageable consistency.

White Sauce and Variations

White sauce is the basis for many sauces, used in dishes such as lasagne and fish pie. The roux method is the 'classic' way to make a white sauce, but the cornflour and microwave methods are both quicker.

The roux method

25g (1oz) butter (preferably unsalted)
3 tbsp plain flour
300ml (11fl oz) milk

Melt the butter in a saucepan, add the flour and stir to make a paste (the roux). Cook gently for 2–3 minutes until the roux starts to bubble.

Remove the pan from the heat and add a little of the milk. Stir (with a spoon or a whisk) until the mixture is smooth. Gradually add the rest of the milk, stirring or whisking all the time to prevent lumps forming. Return the pan to the heat and bring to the boil, still stirring.

Keep the sauce just about at boiling point (and keep stirring) until it has finished thickening, plus another 1–2 minutes, to make sure it's completely cooked.

The cornflour method

300ml (11fl oz) milk
2 tbsp cornflour

Put almost all the milk (except for 2–3 tbsp) into a pan and bring to the boil. Meanwhile, in a small bowl, mix the remaining milk with the cornflour to make a smooth cream. When the milk is boiling, pour a little of it on to the cornflour mixture and stir well.

Pour all this mixture back into the remaining milk and bring to the boil, stirring (with a spoon or a whisk) all the time to prevent lumps forming. Keep the sauce just about at boiling point (and keep stirring) until it has finished thickening, then cook for another 1–2 minutes, to make sure it's completely cooked.

Tip: *Cornflour blended with a little cold water or milk can be added to any sauce that needs thickening.*

187

The all-in-one microwave method

25g (1oz) butter (preferably unsalted)
3 tbsp plain flour
300ml (11fl oz) milk (at room temperature or lukewarm)

Put the butter into a microwaveable bowl and heat it in the microwave for 20–40 seconds on High until melted. Remove from the microwave and add the flour and milk. Whisk together vigorously.

   Cook on High for 2–4 minutes, stopping every 30 seconds to whisk again, until the sauce is thick and thoroughly hot. Give it a final whisk before serving.

Options

• When making a savoury sauce, you can replace up to half the milk with stock.
• If you want a thinner sauce, add a little more milk, stock or water at the end.

Variations on plain white sauce

Once you can make a plain white sauce you'll find it easy to adapt the recipe to create more interesting sauces.

Béchamel sauce
This sauce is often used in lasagnes and moussakas. Make the white sauce as on page 187, using a little less milk for a thicker consistency. Add a little grated nutmeg to finish.

Cheese sauce
Make the white sauce as on page 187, then remove from the heat and stir in 50–100g (2–3½oz) grated cheese (depending how cheesy you want the sauce to be). (Don't keep cooking it or the cheese may go stringy.) Add 1 tsp mustard with the flour or cornflour for extra flavour.

Fish sauce
For a sauce to serve with poached fish, use only 150ml (5fl oz) milk for the sauce (so that it is very thick), then, once the fish is cooked, stir 150ml (5fl oz) of the poaching liquid into the sauce.

Further Information

The **Food Standards Agency** (www.food.gov.uk) and **Action on Additives** (www.actiononadditives.com) both have useful information on healthy eating.

The following online discussion forums have a particular focus on baby-led weaning: **www.babyledweaning.com/forum/**; **http://groups.yahoo.com/group/B-LW/**; and the baby-led weaning group on **www.facebook.com**.

About the Authors

Gill Rapley was a health visitor for 20 years and used her masters degree to begin her research into babies' experiences with solid foods.

Tracey Murkett is a freelance writer who followed baby-led weaning with her daughter, now aged five.

Their first book, *Baby-led Weaning: Helping Your Baby to Love Good Food* (Vermilion, 2008), has inspired many families to follow baby-led weaning.

Acknowledgements

We would like to thank the many parents who sent us their thoughts, recipes and photos, as well as the administrators and members of the online forums who helped to generate such an enthusiastic response. Thanks also to our small army of recipe testers and to Philippa Davis of Mudchute Kitchen, London, for the Easy Bread recipe.

Special thanks go to Carol Williams (of the Infant Feeding Consortium and the Institute of Child Health, University of London) for nutritional advice, to Judith Bird, Jessica Figueras, Lydia Hoult, Elizabeth Mayo, Derrick Murkett and Sarah Squires for their insights on the manuscript, and to our agent, Clare Hulton, and our editors, Julia Kellaway and Louise Coe, for their patience. And, of course, huge thanks to our partners and families, for their long-suffering support.

Index